HEIDEGGER

PHILOSOPHY,

AND POLITICS

HEIDEGGER, PHILOSOPHY, AND POLITICS

THE HEIDELBERG CONFERENCE

JACQUES DERRIDA, HANS-GEORG GADAMER,

AND PHILIPPE LACOUE-LABARTHE

Edited by MIREILLE CALLE-GRUBER

Translated by JEFF FORT

Fordham University Press   *New York 2016*

This book was originally published in French as Jacques Derrida, Hans-Georg Gadamer, and Philippe Lacoue-Labarthe, *La conférence de Heidelberg (1988): Heidegger, Portée philosophique et politique de sa pensée*, Copyright © Lignes, 2014.

Ouvrage publié avec le concours du Ministère français chargé de la Culture–Centre National du Livre.

This work has been published with the assistance of the French Ministry of Culture–National Center for the Book.

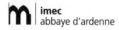

Fordham University Press has no responsibility for the persistence or accuracy of URLs for external or third-party Internet websites referred to in this publication and does not guarantee that any content on such websites is, or will remain, accurate or appropriate.

Fordham University Press also publishes its books in a variety of electronic formats. Some content that appears in print may not be available in electronic books.

Visit us online at www.fordhampress.com.

Library of Congress Cataloging-in-Publication Data available online at http://catalog .loc.gov.

Printed in the United States of America

18 17 16   5 4 3 2 1

First edition

CONTENTS

FOREWORD

Jean-Luc Nancy

The document published here is already equipped with an entire apparatus of presentation and commentary, and it might appear indecent to add to them. But it is with good reason that Michel Surya, coeditor of this volume with the Institut Mémoires de l'édition contemporaine (IMEC), has taken care to situate this publication within the context of its appearance now, in 2014, twenty-six years after the Heidelberg conference took place. He has asked me to write a note to this effect. Although I did not participate in the encounter in Heidelberg, it happens that the three participants who engaged in that debate are no longer with us. My links with two of them, and my relation in general with the work of Heidegger, permit me to risk a response to this request.

The length of time that separates us from 1988 is now much greater than the twelve years that separated that encounter from the death of Heidegger. This time has brought with it a history more and more freighted with profound mutations and with sequels that are less foreseeable than ever; the requirements thus placed on thought are continually changing. At the same time, Heidegger's posthumous publications have progressed considerably and have continued to stoke debates that, for their part, are not always making progress.

It is inevitable that, in 2014, a reading of these exchanges from 1988 reveals a certain dislocation. I will not attempt to analyze this. But one might well assume that, at a moment when Heidegger's

Schwarze Hefte are being published, some readers will not fail to
cast judgments on the relative candor of the arguments of 1988 in
light of the anti-Semitic statements that we can now read in those
notebooks (at the same time as we read there a declaration against
anti-Semitism). In fact, I believe it is necessary to distinguish two
things:

> — on the one hand, it is certain that the absence, in Heidegger's pub-
> lished work, of any explicit argument in favor of what Peter Trawny
> calls "historial anti-Semitism" indeed reveals a disparity or a distor-
> tion that must be interrogated;[1]
> — on the other hand, it is no less certain that this revelation does
> not alter the essential point in what was already discussed in
> 1988—namely, Heidegger's very nearly total silence on "Auschwitz."
> To speak of this silence was already to speak of what is therefore
> not a "revelation" that could be compared to that of an unpunished
> crime.

There are therefore two distinct tasks today: one is to understand why Heidegger reserved this "historial anti-Semitism" for his
personal notes, which, however, he himself wished to have published posthumously; the other is to examine further the separation
between what Heidegger was prepared to think—or to indicate in
thought—from what he was incapable of discerning.

What he was prepared to think finds itself condensed here in
Hans-Georg Gadamer's phrase when he says that "*l'être*" (being),
with the definite article, "is already a falsification."[2] This is a perfect
way to designate the essential resource of this thought. It was not
brought back into the discussion because this was not the immediate objective, but it should always be recalled whenever it is a question of discussing Heidegger. For if one's point of departure is "*être*"
(being), without an article, one can no longer proceed—at least not
in the same way—down the path of that "forgetting of being [*oubli
de l'être*]" that so obsessed and clouded Heidegger's thinking that
it led him to lump together in that "forgetting" the most banal *doxa*

regarding capitalism and technics, the exhaustion of the West and the designation of a pernicious agent called "Jew," thus following a culture that had forged for itself the scapegoat demanded by its secret self-repulsion. That is what one can read in particular in the remarks made by Gadamer and Lacoue-Labarthe, and Derrida's interrogation of the very idea of "responsibility" is related to this.

At the same time, the absence of anti-Semitism in the published texts remains to be analyzed. Everything happened as if Heidegger were aware of the secondary character—the simply "categorial" or empirical but somehow not "existential" character—of something that only configured the devastating power of "forgetting" in a transitory way. But by this very fact he perhaps also had a form of humility or of shame in interrogating publicly the reasons for this configuration: why "the Jews" as bearers of "forgetting"? (Somewhat as for Hegel, they were the people reserved for the testimony of the "unhappy consciousness"; but Hegel wrote this in his public philosophical texts.) One can only conclude the following: Heidegger was not capable of taking account of the historical configuration of anti-Semitism because its "historiality" (its "destinality") prevented him from doing so.

This is indeed attested by the fact that, in the published texts (or in the courses), "historial anti-Semitism" is designated in a way that is visible only in its absence—that is, in the exclusive domination of the Greek origin. In this regard, as well, the Heidelberg debate does not lack indications, although obviously the elements to which we now have access were not available. But if we follow throughout this debate the insistence on the motifs of "destiny" and "history," *historial* we recognize the elements of a reflection that henceforth falls to us: how it is that Heidegger's anti-Semitism—and everything related to it—depends profoundly on a "historial" vision that, despite everything, we must resolve to call more flatly "historicist" (and for which he had no exclusive privilege—far from it!); further, how it is that such a vision (which perhaps remains a "world picture," a *Weltbild*) misrecognizes the thought opened by the suppression of the article before "being [*être*]" and by what leads from there toward a thinking of *Ereignis*. For perhaps the latter has nothing to do with a destinality engaged solely by the Greeks but everything to do with a different history, one that includes Roman, Judeo-Christian, and "modern" events in a sense that Heidegger was perhaps never truly capable of apprehending.

However much time has passed, one thing remains certain and continues to be confirmed: there is no sense in judging Heidegger except on the condition of judging, along with him, ourselves and our history.

PREFACE

Reiner Wiehl

The present volume is the trace of a memorable discussion. It took place on the evening of February 5, 1988, at the University of Heidelberg, in the large lecture hall 13 of the Neue Aula, reserved for exceptional events. It brought together on that occasion Jacques Derrida, Hans-Georg Gadamer, and Philippe Lacoue-Labarthe. In response to an invitation from the organizers, I accepted the role of moderator; as readers will note, my interventions remained strictly within the limits of this task.

This Heidelberg debate was an event that inspired in the public an extraordinary and intense expectation. The cause of this was, above all, the encounter of two world-renowned philosophers. A first debate had already taken place between Derrida and Gadamer in Paris in 1981, and on that occasion they were far from reaching unanimity on the subject under discussion, "Text and Interpretation."[1] It was therefore all the more legitimate to wonder, not without some curiosity, which directions would be taken at present, almost seven years later, in an attempt to reach some level of agreement between a philosophical hermeneutics and a deconstructive critique of logocentrism—a prospect that promised to be rather difficult. But the real question, the one that introduced high tension into the lecture hall, was different: a few months before the meeting in Heidelberg, Victor Farias's *Heidegger et le nazisme* had been published in Paris.[2] This book put on display Heidegger's terrifying connections with the Nazi state and exposed to the public certain details gathered together for the first time in such a massive way. The central question that evening was therefore going to bear, in that immense lecture hall, on the way in which the three philosophers, all profoundly indebted to the work of Heidegger, would be able to face Heidegger's implication in Nazism, and how they would explain and evaluate his silence, a silence never broken, concerning the crimes of the dictatorship of the Third Reich.

EVENT OF THE ARCHIVE

Mireille Calle-Gruber

The event took place: it was a great moment of explication (*Auseinandersetzung*) and of truth(s) between Hans-Georg Gadamer, Jacques Derrida, and Philippe Lacoue-Labarthe.[1] It was transmitted, recorded, photographed, filmed by television (Westdeutscher Rundfunk), and commented on by special correspondents from numerous newspapers. Then retranscribed, corrected by each one of the participants, reread by Derrida, whom Gadamer had asked to review his own interventions. The text of the public debate, and of the meeting with the journalists the following day, was ready. But we agreed, all of us, to defer publication: to wait for tensions to subside, along with the noise of the media's uncontrolable effects.

From that moment, what is reaching us today, twenty-five years later, is the event of the archive—*in truth*. Which is to say that it is a question of the political (*arkheion* designates the house of the archontes that had the function of preserving official documents). More ample than memory, the archive is not turned toward the past: its gesture is inscribed in the present of reading and of writing and is a call for the future-to-come [*l'à-venir*]. The event of the archive, or that which inaugurates life in its futurity, life-to-come, *in truth*. That is what the pages that follow give us to think. In this year 2014, when the violences of various nationalisms and extreme right elements are striving, with a certain success, to infiltrate institutions, such a reading of politico-philosophical interrogations is far

from idle. Likewise for the exemplarity of an ethical will to dialogue
and solidarity, despite the divergences that clearly emerged among
the three participants.

When the debate between Hans-Georg Gadamer, Jacques Derrida, and Philippe Lacoue-Labarthe was held at the University of Heidelberg, on February 5, 1988, under the official title, "Heidegger:
Portée philosophique et politique de sa pensée" (Heidegger: Philosophical and Political Dimensions of his Thought), the context was
volatile in every respect. I was able to help bring about this meeting thanks to the friendship of Philippe Lacoue-Labarthe; he made
the connection with Derrida, whom I did not yet know, and who
agreed immediately, with the inexhaustible generosity that I would
continue to find in him. It was also thanks to the confidence shown
to me by Gadamer, at the time an emeritus professor who continued to give a very well-attended seminar at the University of Heidelberg.[2] As for Reiner Wiehl, professor of philosophy at Heidelberg
and a former assistant to Gadamer, we had already had occasion to
work together, and it was obvious that it would be ideal for him to
preside over the session.

The year 1988 was a period of intense polemics. To be sure, these
polemics were stoked by the publication in 1987 of the French edition of Victor Farias's book *Heidegger and Nazism*, a rather sim-
plistic work that garnered much attention in the media. But the
polemics had deeper sources, having to do with the political repressed in France: anti-Semitism, collaboration, the Resistance, the
crimes of the Vichy regime. This was the period when Robert Faurisson's revisionist theses were on display, as were the negationist
statements denying the existence of the extermination camps. The
Barbie trial had taken place; there was the "Paul de Man affair" and
the appearance of Derrida's book *Memoirs for Paul de Man*, first in
English (Columbia University Press, 1986), then in French in an ex-
panded edition (Galilée, 1988). Philippe Lacoue-Labarthe had just
published *Heidegger, Art and Politics* (*La fiction du politique: Heidegger, l'art et la politique* [Paris: Bourgois, 1987]), which included

an appendix, "On Victor Farias' Book," and Jean-Luc Nancy published *The Inoperative Community* (*La communauté désoeuvrée* [Paris: Bourgois 1986, 1988]), which elaborated an analysis of the process of "mythation" in the West; this came after the work co-authored by Nancy and Lacoue-Labarthe on "The Nazi Myth" first presented at Schiltigheim for a colloquium on "The Mechanisms of Fascism," organized in 1980 by the "Comité d'information sur l'holocauste."[3] Their analyses studied the way in which, at the heart of the political and social practice of Nazism, myth was set to work as an identitary figure leading to the fashioning of a people according to a supposed Germano-Aryan autochthony, and how the Nazi horror was based on a "national aestheticism"—a term thus designating, as Lacoue-Labarthe specified in *Heidegger, Art and Politics*, the symptom of the "aborted Modern"—within a modern politics that, far from acceding to the modern, remained subjected to the *imitatio* of the ancient, to the "Greek model."

In addition, while not exactly polemical, the encounter that had taken place a few years earlier between Gadamer and Derrida—in the context of the colloquium "Texte et interprétation" organized by Philippe Forget at the Goethe Institute in Paris (April 25–27, 1981)—had quickly become contentious, and the two philosophers found themselves at odds with one another. Whereas Gadamer, following the hermeneutic approach, pursued a philosophical thought of continuity and articulation, Derrida was already proceeding along the path of interruption, an attempt to "give to read the interruption that in any case will decide the figure itself,"[4] according to an approach whose formulation—"I must teach you how to teach me how to read myself"—soon stood as a counterpoint to Gadamer's "understanding." And Derrida, with "Good Will to Power," offered a "Response to Hans-Georg Gadamer," who for his part titled his "Response to Jacques Derrida": "And Yet: Power of Good Will."[5] With this debate in Heidelberg, one might anticipate that these tensions would hardly be calmed by the presence of Lacoue-Labarthe, this thinker who, with great urgency, sought to expose "the historial caesura of our time" that Auschwitz represents,[6] and the discordant temporality of a humanity henceforth "caesura-ed" ("what follows the caesura will never be the same as what went before; the end will never again resemble the beginning");[7] at the same time, Gadamer opened the proceedings by insisting on the "task of *communicating*," which he considered a philosophical imperative, and he made it a point to take up the dialogue *beginning from* the impasse where they had left off in 1981.[8]

This is to say that, on February 5, 1988, a reflection on the philosophical and political dimensions of Heidegger's thought had become a very current and pressing matter. To this was added the fact that it was in the very lecture hall where Heidegger, in 1933, as rector of the University of Freiburg, had given the speech on "The University in the New Reich" that this debate was to take place, before more than a thousand students and professors who were summoned to their responsibility to *think thinking.*

The encounter of 1988 was no doubt rendered historic by the *kairos* of this moment, in which the magnitude of the participants rose to the level of the situation of crisis touching directly on the task of thought. But above all, this encounter is important *at present*, in *our* present, because of the lesson that it offers concerning the political and ethical stakes that traverse our existences: allowing us to rework a past that continues to make demands on us and whose unsaid elements burden the future, and to elaborate, in the order of events, the emergence of a thought capable, perhaps, of thinking an always fragile democracy.

That is why we must be careful here not to hypostasize the scene, still less to sacralize it; it must come to us anew, enlivened by its ambivalences and uncertainties: the event in its multiple echoes, in the trembling of its becoming.

In this year of 2014, our vigilance can only increase, given the publication of the first three volumes of the Heidegger's *Schwarze Hefte*.[9] Not that one must interpret the Heidelberg conference on the basis of these "black notebooks," whose existence was unknown to everyone at the time; to do so would falsely distort the 1988 debate. But the *Schwarze Hefte* that Heidegger kept from the early 1930s until the beginning of the 1970s, in parallel to his published works, promise to shed light on the divergences that appear, at the darkest moment of German history in the twentieth century, between the public works and these working notes, which the philosopher held back for a much later publication, as the concluding moment of his complete works, the *Gesamtausgabe*.

The *Schwarze Hefte* revive the question of the anti-Semitism that has been attributed to Heidegger. At the time of the Heidelberg conference, this consisted only of one isolated incident related by Karl Jaspers, concerning an anti-Semitic remark made during a private conversation in May 1933, that had no echo in Heidegger's published works.[10] Now Peter Trawny, the editor of the *Schwarze Hefte*, speaks of a "historial anti-Semitism" (*"seinsgeschichtlicher Antisemitismus"*) in reference to certain passages of the notebooks.[11]

In that light, Derrida's position in 1988, calling for a "polemical relation" of "counter-questioning" with regard to Heidegger, will no doubt be more necessary than ever, so as not to hastily conclude the debate by reducing Heidegger to an ordinary Nazi, or even to a meta-Nazi. As it stands, any critical reading of these new documents would have to define what they contain in terms of anti-Semitic remarks, but also in terms of the ambivalences in their formulations, or else to establish the distinction made there between "vulgar National Socialism" and "spiritual national Socialism," while also taking account of the deconstructive argumentation that Heidegger brings to the question of being in general (which he crosses out), and on the forms of Christian and Jewish monotheism in particular, considered as strategies of domination (his anticlerical position is well known).[12] The task of critique today, then, is to pose questions precisely where Heidegger's questioning failed—that is, to take up questions at the place where Heidegger's thought re-

mained incomplete, in the hiatus in which his ethical failure is inscribed, his unforgivable silence regarding Auschwitz. It is this place
that all the protagonists of the Heidelberg debate designate as the
point where they must exercise *their responsibility*—which is to say,
ours, as Jean-Luc Nancy rightly reminds us in his note from 2014
which serves as the Foreword to this book.

When Gadamer died on March 13, 2002, at the age of 102, Derrida wrote a text that was much more than a circumstantial hom-
age: "I do not believe in the death of Gadamer. I cannot bring myself to believe in it. I had gotten used to the idea that Gadamer
would never die, that he was not a man who could die. . . . I en-
vied him his capacity to affirm life. It seemed invincible. I was convinced that someone like Gadamer deserved never to die, because
we needed such an absolute witness, who participated actively or
as an observer in all the philosophical debates of the century."[13]
Aside from being a beautiful salute to life, which was not so custom-
ary for him, Derrida also underscored the unconditional respect
they had always shared, despite the gulf separating their interpretations of interpretation, and stressed that there was "no danger that
war, contempt or insult"[14] would ever disturb what bound them
across such a distance.

That is indeed what one hears in the Heidelberg encounter, beyond the misunderstandings and impasses: the certainty, and the
promise, of a respect owed to the exigency of thought. Gadamer
and Derrida, and Lacoue-Labarthe with them, affirm in what follows
the injunction placed on their responsibility "before the necessity of
reading Heidegger as he did not read himself."[15]

But there is more. For in this posthumous address we see that
Derrida, performing the same gesture made by Gadamer in Heidelberg, speaks here again *beginning from* their disagreement in 1981.
And he cites the text with which his interlocutor had replied ("And
yet: the power of good will"), as if it had made its way to him, finally
audible, by approaching a certain process of depropriation:

Every reading that seeks understanding is only a step on a path that
never ends. Whoever sets out on this path knows that he or she will
never be completely done with the text: one accepts the blow, the
thrust, that the text delivers. The fact that a poetic text can so touch
someone that one ends up "entering" into it and recognizing oneself
in it, assumes neither harmonious agreement nor self-confirmation.
One must lose oneself in order to find oneself. I believe I am not
very far from Derrida, when I stress that one never knows in advance
what one will find oneself to be.[16]

One year later, on February 15, 2003,[17] during a lecture given by
Derrida in memory of Gadamer, once again in Heidelberg, it was
in the reading of a poem that he found the promise of encounter. I am referring to "Rams," with its subtitle that gestures toward
Gadamer: "Uninterrupted Dialogue—Between Two Infinities, the
Poem."[18] The poem is by Paul Celan ("Grosse, glühende Wölbung,"
in *Atemwende*), in which one verse in particular calls for interpretation: "Die Welt is fort, ich muss dich tragen," "The world is gone,
I must carry you."[19] Here it is a question of the task of "carrying
the other," of the need to carry him, "to carry without appropriat-
ing."[20] "And I only am, I can only be, I *must* only be starting from
this strange, dislocated bearing of the infinitely other in me."[21] And
it is indeed in the relation to the poem that the two philosophers
echo one another: for in the end Gadamer was always attentive to
the question of translation as poetic experience[22] and considered
poetry as "the great instance for the experience of the ownness and
foreignness of language."[23]

During the evening of the debate on Heidegger, on February 5,
1988, the encounter took place under the sign of hospitality: a hospitality in the French language, offered by Gadamer to his guests.
Thus were all three of them strangers and foreigners, Derrida and
Lacoue-Labarthe in Germany, Gadamer in the French language, and
all three were "others" in depropriation and in the need to "carry
the other." The force of this dialogue on the edge of the abyss and in

an awareness of the untranslatable is also, for us today, a precious lesson. It obliges us to rework questions that remain urgently open, incessantly reemerging in the languages of writing-thinking. And to implicate ourselves.

After Jacques Derrida's death on October 9, 2004, but just before the collection published in Montreal was to appear the following year, Jean Grondin carried out a symbolic gesture of philosophy's infinite conversation: he translated Derrida's German text into French ("Comme il avait raison! Mon Cicérone Hans-Georg Gadamer") and placed it in that collection, thus giving a supplementary turn of the screw. Between two infinities, interrupting the interruption. Philippe Lacoue-Labarthe died on January 28, 2007, in Paris. Reiner Wiehl, with whom we were planning to publish the present volume, died in Heidelberg on December 30, 2010, a few weeks after sending me the text of his preface. My gratitude goes out to Andrea Gadamer, to Marguerite Derrida, and to Claire Lacoue-Labarthe, who authorized this publication.[24]

To make known today the words of these three philosophers, their texts, their exemplary effort of justice and of precision [*justesse*] takes on a singular weight. The works remain vigilant; they help us to discern events *in truth*. They remind us that "we no longer live in the dimension or in the logic of the origin. We exist in belatedness, in a historical after-effect [*l'après-coup*]. Which does not mean that the extremity of the belated is not also the emergence of the new. It is even precisely this that we are required to think."[25] These words of Philippe Lacoue-Labarthe and Jean-Luc Nancy open the threshold of "The Nazi Myth." They are more than ever a part of our actuality.

The injunction addressed to us today by the Heidelberg conference is exorbitant: to strive to read Heidegger as he did not read himself—that is, rather than limiting ourselves to condemning him, to make it such that his silence on Auschwitz carries us toward the difficult courage of thinking.

HEIDEGGER, PHILOSOPHY, AND POLITICS

Jacques
DERRIDA
(Paris)

Hans-Georg
GADAMER
(Heidelberg)

Philippe
LACOUE-LABARTHE
(Strasbourg)

discutent sur

HEIDEGGER

PORTEE PHILOSOPHIQUE ET POLITIQUE DE SA PENSEE

Président de séance:
Reiner WIEHL (Heidelberg)

Vendredi 5 février 1988,
20 Uhr c.t., Hörsaal 13,
Neue Universität, Heidelberg
La discussion se déroulera
en français

Présentation: Mireille Calle-Gruber

Informations
Institut Français
Seminarstraße 3
6900 Heidelberg
tél. 06221 / 25288

Philosophisches Seminar

et

Institut Français
Heidelberg

INVITATION

En collaboration avec le DAAD de Heidelberg
et les Services Culturels de l'Ambassade de France

HEIDELBERG, FEBRUARY 5, 1988

NEUE UNIVERSITÄT, HS 13

CONFERENCE OF FEBRUARY 5, 1988

MIREILLE CALLE-GRUBER: On June 30, 1933, in the Neue Aula of this same building, Heidegger, at the time the rector of Freiburg University, and since *Sein und Zeit* on his way to achieving world-wide recognition, gave a speech with the title "The University in the New Reich." There was such a large crowd that it became necessary to transmit audio of the speech into another room nearby—as is the case again this evening. Among the listeners was Karl Jaspers, who would later remark, in his *Philosophical Autobiography*:

> As to form it was a masterful speech, as to content it presented a program of National Socialist renewal for the universities. He demanded a total change of the essence of spirit. The majority of professors then holding positions were incapable of accomplishing this new task. In ten years, a new generation of competent academics

would be formed. In the meantime, it would be a transitional period. He railed against many aspects of university life, including the high salaries. For this he received thunderous applause from the students and even from a few of the professors. I sat in the front row, at the end, my legs stretched out in front of me and my hands in my pockets, completely still.[1]

This story from Karl Jaspers, describing himself in contrast with the enthusiasm aroused by the program of National-Socialist renewal, says a great deal—or too little—about the atmosphere of that time.

Two accounts of Heidegger's intervention appeared in the newspapers, one in the *Heidelberger Neueste Nachrichten*, which Guido Schneeberger republished in his collection, the other in the *Heidelberger Student*, in which the author of the piece is pleased to report "that the words of the speaker did not disappoint the audience and that these words grasped profoundly what is coming to pass in our time [*das Geschehen der Zeit*] and indicated with clear certainty [*mit klarer Sicherheit*] what is in the process of becoming [*das Werdende*]." As for the text of this speech itself, it was never published, contrary to what the book by Victor Farias, *Heidegger and Nazism*, may claim on this point.

I evoke these details as a reminder. More precisely, I evoke them because this location—Heidelberg, the university—is itself a memory that charges this evening's encounter with a singular significance. As a reminder, then, more than as a way to evoke again a controversial book, the one by Farias, whose errors, not to mention the dishonesty of its conflations, have been denounced by a number of French philosophers, whereas others, particularly Jürgen Habermas, consider it important and, despite its faults, true regarding the essentials.

But what, truly, is essential here? That is indeed the crucial question, and we see clearly enough that a compilation of facts is not sufficient for grasping what is at stake. For if, when

it comes to the revisionist theses, it is necessary to have the political vigilance of Habermas, the problem *for thought* becomes
all the more complex when it is posed in the following way: how
was it possible for a thinker who is considered to be the greatest
philosopher of our time to have engaged in the National-Socialist
movement? And still more grave: how could one be silent on his
postwar silence, and how could one accept that he never publicly
retracted what he had said, thus failing to think the greatest horror that has ever been—the industrial extermination of the Jews?

Could one minimize such a fault and, like Jean Beaufret,
separate the man from his work (which Marcuse refused to do)?
Hans-Georg Gadamer, in a recent piece published by *Le Nouvel
Observateur*, is categorical:

> Did he then feel no responsibility for the terrible consequences of
> Hitler's seizure of power, the new barbarism, the Nuremberg laws,
> the terror, the blood spilled—and, finally, the indelible shame of the
> extermination camps? The answer is a rigorous no.[2]

There is no doubt that in a few moments the debate will take
up this concept of responsibility, especially given that the author
of those words has indicated to me that the article, precisely on
this point, was truncated.

This is indeed the path of reflection opened in recent years
by writings that interrogate the responsibility of thought—that is,
that enter into a debate with Heidegger's thought and *in the terms
of* this thought. It is there that Jacques Derrida's book *Of Spirit:
Heidegger and the Question* is inscribed, as is that of Philippe
Lacoue-Labarthe, *Heidegger, Art and Politics: The Fiction of the
Political*, among others. And in Germany, in addition to the recent
book by Karl Löwith, *Mein Leben in Deutschland vor und nach
1933*,[3] there are studies by Otto Pöggeler, Hugo Ott, and Bernd
Martin. Paradoxically, one discovers thus that it is *through* the
thought of Heidegger, and through this process of the *Auseinan-*

dersetzung whose name he fashioned, that one can attempt to
understand—I quote Jacques Derrida—"what *avoiding* means"
and "where spirit escapes deconstruction" and can attempt to
think the Nazi crime in its specificity—that is to say, to think the
unthinkable: the apocalypse of Auschwitz where, as Hannah
Arendt has written, "something happened to which we cannot
reconcile ourselves."

Finally, for France today there are perhaps other questions,
as well. The incredible agitation the Heidegger "case" has caused
there for a few months now, and the passions it has aroused, are
no doubt related to the fact that the French are in the process
of settling their own accounts with a past that they have never
thought through—Vichy, collaboration—and that has resurfaced
recently during the Barbie trial, where the anticipated debate was
avoided. But one thinks also of the revisionist positions of Robert
Faurisson and of the Henri Roques affair; of the Jankélévitch-
Sartre affair; and, most recently, of the letters from Beaufret to
Faurisson, published in *Le Monde*, that undermine the image of
the Resistance.[4]

In this respect, there is in Lacoue-Labarthe's book a terrible
sentence: "Nazism is a humanism insofar as it rests upon a deter-
mination of *humanitas* which is . . . more powerful,"[5] a sentence
that says clearly enough that the Nazi crime is neither a museum
object nor the fault of the Other, but that it reveals the totalitarian
essence of our Occident.

We can appreciate, then, the extent to which the dialogue
to be engaged this evening constitutes an important moment in
the advancement of these questions. It is all the more significant
in that it integrates two elements that I would like to mention in
conclusion: on the one hand, this encounter hearkens back to
the one that took place in Paris, in 1981, between Gadamer and
Derrida, and that since then has remained without a sequel. On
the other hand, its significance is increased today by a double
gesture: that of Jacques Derrida and of Philippe Lacoue-Labarthe,

who have agreed to come here for this discussion, here to Germany and to this university whose importance I recalled a moment
ago, and the reciprocal gesture of Hans-Georg Gadamer and of
Reiner Wiehl, who from the outset offered to cross into the linguistic territory of French—a generous gesture for which I am infinitely
grateful to them, since, without it, this encounter could not have
taken place. The force of thought also lies in its exposition; if the
discussion had required the intermediary of a translator, it would
have had neither the same sincerity nor the same intensity.

This tolerance and this welcoming of the language of the
other, which are also yours since so many of you have come to
follow this discussion in French, manifest the will to open a dialogue in all its gravity. In short, it is for this openness, which is so
emblematic, that I would like to sincerely thank the four participants, certainly, and all of you here.

REINER WIEHL: I will add only a few words to this excellent
introduction by Mireille Calle-Gruber, to whom I express my
gratitude for having organized this encounter, which is, for all of
us, an exceptional occasion. I would also like to extend a warm
welcome to our French colleagues, Jacques Derrida and Philippe
Lacoue-Labarthe, whose presence offers the possibility of a discussion between French and German philosophers. I would like
to welcome as well the great master of the Heidelberg School,
Professor Gadamer. Mireille Calle-Gruber has indicated in a very
expressive way, I think, why the Heidegger case causes us such
disquiet today—and will no doubt continue to do so, I am sure, in
years to come. But regarding this Heidegger case, the stature and
the knowledge of our guests guarantee us that reflections of the
highest order will be devoted to it, and that the problem of the
political will be situated on a philosophical plane—and this is of
great importance.

As for the organization of the debate, I would say . . . that
there is no organization. There is the reality of this discussion,

which we are now beginning, and for which we will give ourselves time: all the time necessary. It will last one hour and a half, perhaps more. When the "combatants" are tired, we will take a break, before opening the discussion to the public.

HANS-GEORG GADAMER: I am very grateful to my friend Reiner Wiehl for having already conveyed what is most important: that is, our thanks to our guests, and to the audience for their presence and their attention. We must also ask forgiveness for our French, which is not very pleasant to your ears. I have never lived in a French-speaking country. This is not my fault: it is the history of the world that has prevented it from being otherwise. It is therefore only a French learned at school that I am using here, a French from before the war—the First World War.

I proposed that we hold this conversation in French for, I believe, there is no authentic conversation without dialogism, that is, without the basis of a common language. Hence my decision. And I am grateful that our friends who have come from France have agreed to suffer listening to our pronunciation and our stammering. That is also the reason why I have no text: my French would not be sufficient to the task. It would not be sufficient to the basic standards of style. The license permitted to an improvisation is the only way I can introduce myself into this evening's conversation.

To begin, I will recall how I came into contact with M. Derrida and his friends, in Paris. I was already old, indeed I was already retired, when the first books by Derrida were published. I remember perfectly the day I received the book dedicated to M. Beaufret;[6] a book in which I found, for the first time, a French author who was speaking of Heidegger by beginning with Aristotle. I said to myself, well, now, this is something worth reading and examining. For this was also the tune I had forever been singing to my students and colleagues: there is no point in speaking about Heidegger if one is not familiar with the origins of Platonic and Aristotelian metaphysics. That is why I was drawn from the beginning to the publications of Jacques Derrida. And that is why when I studied the first publications, and his point of departure in Husserl in *Voice and Phenomenon*, this reading was in a way a return to my own beginnings—to a period when I was under the first impression of the young Heidegger and of Husserl's *Logical Investigations*, which stimulated me but also provoked me by this abstract Platonism that dealt with the question of meaning-to-say [*le vouloir-dire*]. Later I began if not to understand, then to enter somewhat into the set of problems touching on Heidegger and the different directions in which this thought led us—and how, to some extent, it also determined us.

The characteristic concept of Jacques Derrida's work, *deconstruction*, was for me a provocation of the first order, because I understood immediately how one aspect of the term "*Destruktion*" that resonated in our own ears, in our youth, had in it nothing negative, nothing of a "destroy." "*Destruktion*": at that time, what was being said in this way was a new opening, where things had long been covered over and hidden, falsified by a long history of Latinization and scholastic conceptualization. "Destruction" became the return to living speech. The term "deconstruction," then, taught me immediately to recognize this connotation that had never come to mind for us when we were listening to the young Heidegger speak of *Destruktion*. "Deconstruction" wants, it seems to me, to underscore that it is a question not simply of destroying, but also of constructing something. And I believe that this is true, at least in intention, for Heidegger himself, as for all those who were provoked but also stimulated by his thought. That is also the reason why there are no "Heideggerians." Heidegger said it himself several times, and I believe that he was not wrong: the work done by those who imitate Heidegger has no philosophical value. One can certainly develop perspectives, whether contrary, opposite, or similar to the directions of Heidegger's thought, but one could never proceed in the form of an imitation, no more than of an orthodoxy.

I was therefore ready, in sum, to adapt myself to Jacques Derrida and to his own approach to philosophy. No doubt I am not inhabited, as he is, by the conviction that there is a total rupture of communication among men today. Perhaps I am too superficial, or too optimistic, but I am terribly preoccupied with the task that consists in *communicating* with others—with the youngest, first of all, but with those of my age, as well. This function of rupture seems to me to be one of the concepts that really do constitute a difference from my own approach to philosophical thinking. This has led some to make a distinction by invoking a "hermeneutics of suspicion." And it is true that the hermeneutics that founds my reflection insists on communication and is less interested in the hidden meanings [*sous-entendus*] of words and of discourse.

This was one of the first problems between us, a problem that it is certainly worth discussing. The point on which this divergence is manifest in an almost polemical manner, not with regard to ourselves, but with regard to the interpretation and appraisal called for by Heidegger's thought, is the problem of Nietzsche, at the moment when he plays a determining role in France—that is, after the Second World War. Jacques Derrida sees in Heidegger's interpretation of Nietzsche a form of continuation, unintended and involuntary, of the tradition of metaphysics and even of logocentrism. I confess that this thought of Jacques Derrida was, for me, a true provocation. For in my view it was precisely in this that Heidegger's great merit lay: having taught me that logocentrism was in a way the destiny of the West. That it was at the foundation of metaphysics, especially, of course, in Aristotelian philosophy. That this logocentrism had constituted, for Heidegger himself, the true invitation to philosophy.

Heidegger was no doubt a religious thinker when he began to develop his own concepts and to comprehend something that is

not comprehensible by means of the conceptuality or the metaphysics of the Greeks and of medieval or even modern thinkers. It
was then that he risked this metaphysics of finitude or of *Sein* [be-being
ing], which is a verb, a temporal expression, and not at all something that one could articulate as *das* Sein, *the* Sein: that does not
really make sense. And I believe that on this point Jacques Derrida
is not very far away in his manner of approaching Heidegger. But
perhaps I am underestimating the differences to be found in our
common point of departure, namely Nietzsche.

I must confess that for my part I never had any direct contact with Nietzsche in my youth, and Heidegger himself came to
Nietzsche later, only around 1930. Of course, Nietzsche had a presence for all of us, and when Heidegger in *Sein und Zeit* quotes the
second of the *Untimely Meditations*, this was a common reference
point for all of us. In contrast, the question of the eternal return,
the will to power, the preference for what was in a way incompre-
hensible in the audacious experiments of Nietzsche's writings, all
this had no existence before this second stage in the development
of Heidegger's thought. One of the points of debate will therefore
also be, no doubt, what we tried to discuss a few years ago in Paris,
which concerns the different approaches to Heidegger by way of
his interpretation of Nietzsche.

But this evening we are here not only to debate the phases
and the tendencies toward the death drive encountered and
evinced by a great thinker like Heidegger, but we also want to
take into account this mystery, this problem that has troubled
us for a long time now—and not only since the appearance of a
second-rate book, the book by Farias—namely, Heidegger's engagement in the National-Socialist movement. We were troubled
by it from the moment when we began working with him, when
we were his students. I was at Marburg and was a young colleague
of Heidegger's when he began to get involved in the Nazi movement in Freiburg. It is true, and it must be confessed, that for
many of us this came as a surprise. Perhaps one will say: you were

blind! Young people are blind, in a way, when they are guided by
a master with great energy and force; so they give their attention
only to what corresponds to their own interests and their own
questions. It is true, we were surprised.

But I believe that this surprise must allow us to go further
today; I mean, further than the specific details of this participation of Heidegger in the Nazi movement, whether during his
year as rector, later, or even quite a bit earlier. This surprise must
allow us to pose the crucial and absolutely inevitable problem,
which is, through Heidegger, the problem of German Nazism.
The question obviously demands competencies that I am far from
possessing, and that the historians themselves do not have. But it
is clear that one cannot dissociate Heidegger's philosophy from
the fact of the extermination that took place in the history of our
century. To be sure, Nazism is not a German specialty; there was
fascism; there was also the shifting and continually more bitter
image of the development of the Russian revolution. This is the
background against which, I believe, we must try to understand
also the temptations presented by circumstances in those years;
and of course, no less, the different responses chosen by different people.

There is an entire context that is at issue when today we
discuss the relations between Heidegger's philosophical thought
and its political dimensions—a context that began to orient us in
Germany, after the First War. It was a period (going back before
World War I) of liberalism, of a bourgeois culture that was shaken
and was beginning to totter, when the young poets of Germany
and the artists began already to evoke the terrible visions of
destruction of our culture. This period, as we know, is reflected
perfectly in our literature. In addition, we also see very clearly
how the obvious and undisputed decline of progress that accompanied the period of my education was closely linked with the
formation of our problems, including in philosophy. The critique
of transcendental idealism, of the neo-Kantianism that was domi-

nant during my youth, the critique on the part of Jewish thinkers
and Catholic thinkers during and immediately after the First World
War—this was, in a sense, the background against which the young
Heidegger made his entry, and by which he was determined.

Well, there are no doubt two problems that have remained
very troubling for me throughout my life. The first has to do with
the responsibility assumed by a man as excellent and paradig-
matic as the thinker that Heidegger was in 1933; a responsibility,
notably, with respect to the great number of his young colleagues
and of his students who followed him in his decision. But also,
along with this responsibility, there is the other fact, contradictory
and disturbing: to wit, the *same* thinker, at the *same* moment—at
a time when he supported, certainly not everything, not the anti-
Semitism, not the racism, not the biologism of Nazism, but all the
same some of its fundamental decisions—this thinker was writing
texts that we still today can read as an anticipation of the coming
reality. I am thinking in particular of "Die Zeit des Welbildes,"[7] of
the description of the "forgetting of being," as he called it, of the
predominance of technics and of the consequences of the industrial revolution; in short, of everything that, as we know, began
long ago but became evident only more recently, and is evident for
young people to such a degree that this is perhaps today, in the
eyes of the old man I am now, the most troubling fact there is: I
mean, the pessimism of young people with regard to the possible
future of humanity.

In my view, this is the great ambiguity in the Heidegger case.
There is another one, and that is, obviously, the ambiguity of his
silence. Heidegger never spoke of his error. To be sure, he did
say once that it was "the greatest error of my life," this in reference to his engagement in the Nazi Party. But that is superficial
with regard to the serious affinities that exist between Heidegger's
philosophical position and certain tendencies of that movement.
It is this question that has always preoccupied the Jewish friends
I have met in America during my travels. They all say: the error of

Heidegger, his participation in the movement, these are things that could be forgiven. But why did he never evoke that? Why did he refuse to speak of it?

I have tried, in the article published by *Le Nouvel Observateur*[8]—though it must be said that the text was very mutilated; but what can one expect, when a German writer engages in a Parisian debate: it remains somewhat in the margins, and that is absolutely normal, I am not complaining—, in this article, then, I have tried to explain why Heidegger did not recognize any responsibility. I said that it is because Heidegger thought that it was no longer *his* revolution; it had become a decadent revolution for which he did not feel responsible. This is something that, it seems to me, slightly changes the tune we are in the habit of hearing.

The recent book by Victor Farias, while it produced certain absurdities, was nonetheless pertinent and correct on one point: I am referring to the date of June 30, 1934, the Night of the Long Knives. It was there that my difference with Heidegger, I believe, revealed itself as fundamental. For both of us, this was a date with fatal consequences, but we did not understand this fatality in the same way. For Heidegger, it was the end of the revolution as he understood it: that is to say, a spiritual and philosophical revolution that ought to have brought with it a renewal of humanity in all of Europe. Whereas for me this stabilization of the Nazi revolution through the support of the army brought the irrevocable certainty that it would never be possible to be liberated from this regime without a catastrophe. This was, in my eyes, the prospect we were facing. And for me it is clear that it is mere hypocrisy to ask, why did you not rebel against it? When faced with weapons one does not counter them with preaching.

These, you see, are the problems—and on this point I will stop—engendered by the political impact, the political decisions and facts that accompanied our reception of the radical thought of Heidegger. These are the diverse paths by which we tried, each one of us, to develop our own conclusions. In that article, mutilated as it was, I also tried to sketch out how I myself drew certain conclusions from this. That attempt will no doubt appear, in the eyes of my colleague Derrida, to derive from an optimism that is too naive: for I think that communication can always take place, and that in my work there is not at all this insistence on the *rupture* that formed the destiny of human culture today. I do not underestimate this difference between us, and I hope to learn much this evening as to the possibilities of establishing relations between two perspectives, each of which is, it seems to me, that of a man who is sincere and decisive.

RW: Thank you, Mr. Gadamer. I can only suppose that our French colleagues find this situating of the context quite thought-provoking and that they wish to respond. I turn to them without further ado.

JACQUES DERRIDA: I am very happy—and in a moment I will tell you why I am also afraid. I am very impressed, very intimidated by what is developing here. I will try to explain this in a moment. First I would like to thank Mireille Calle-Gruber and all those who organized this encounter, Professor Wiehl, and Professor Gadamer for the very generous words he just offered.

I will come back to what you said a moment ago about the choice of language because naturally our gratitude, I think, on the part of Philippe Lacoue-Labarthe and myself, as well as all those here whose mother tongue is French, our gratitude is altogether singular, and I wish to insist on this for a moment. There is indeed a certain irony—when one thinks for example of what Heidegger in an interview with *Der Spiegel* said about the possibility, or not, of thinking in a Latin language—in our coming together here this evening to speak of him; and I imagine his specter, or something of his specter, predicting that this evening *there will be no thinking [ça ne pensera pas]*! And that is indeed what may happen.

Why am I afraid? First, because the agreement we came to in preparation, or rather in non-preparation, for this meeting, was an agreement in favor of improvisation: we are improvising, and we will continue to improvise. Why improvise in this case? Whereas everything, on the contrary—the gravity of the matter, the complexity of the problems, of the texts, of the political and historical situations, of the traps awaiting us at every moment—all this, precisely, would push us to weigh our words, to leave nothing to chance, to never improvise. And I must say that personally, each time that I have attempted to speak of these questions—as I have done again recently—, I avoided improvisation as much as I possibly could. Not in order simply to defend or protect myself, but because the consequences of every phrase and sentence are so grave that all this deserves, precisely, to be removed from the element of improvisation.

And yet, like everyone here, I have not only given my agreement but also have asked that the encounter be improvised. Why? This evening I think we are going to speak a great deal about responsibility. Professor Gadamer has already abundantly addressed this; and a question required in advance, precisely a philosophical question, will be to know in what terms responsibility will be defined. Which category of responsibility ought to guide us, not only in the definition but in the taking of responsibilities? When faced with these responsibilities that must be taken, why accept and agree to improvise? Because I believe that in the face of what has just happened in Germany and in France—and I am referring here to a sequence of a few months, since the publication of a certain number of texts, that of Farias, of Lacoue-Labarthe, and of others—, the reactions have taken this form (among others): many of those who were not professional philosophers, or experts on Heidegger, if you will, and who suddenly discovered, notably with Farias's book, things they did not suspect, have accused those who have been interested in Heidegger either of being uninformed regarding Heidegger's Nazi engagement or, if they were informed, of not having exhibited in the public arena, of not having transformed into a common problem, what they were aware of as professional philosophers.

And I believe that the importance of Farias's book may lie in this. There are some of us here who have, each in his own way, formulated very well-grounded reservations, I think, on many aspects of the work Farias has done. I will not go back over this now. He is not here, and it would be necessary, in order to reopen this problem, to look very closely at a certain number of texts—which we are unable to do in the conditions in which we find ourselves this evening. I would like to underscore, rather, the importance of this book, and to ask what this importance might consist in.

This book, because of a certain number of documents that it deals with more or less correctly, but that it brings together in a sort of montage, or synopsis, which had not yet been placed before a public of nonprofessional philosophers in this form, has naturally provoked the emotion you are aware of, and has obliged . . .—and I consider that this provocation is not only negative: it has been negative in certain aspects, but not only negative—, has forced professional philosophers to explain themselves in a more urgent, more immediate manner, and to do so in forums that they have habitually avoided taking part in, by speaking and improvising. And I consider that this urgency, whatever risk it may entail, and has entailed, regarding the complexity of the matter in question, regarding the dimension of certain problems—this urgency is not simply negative. I believe that improvising runs the risk of preventing us (and this is why I am afraid), of preventing the philosophers and teachers that we are—because of the format of this meeting, the large audience in its quality and its quantity—from maintaining a certain refinement, a certain rhythm in the discussion that we are used to. In short, a certain style of discussion that is ours. I am afraid, because of the lights, the microphones, the audience, because of your expectations, that certain effects will be reproduced, effects that I evoked a moment ago.

And yet, I believe that it was necessary to take this risk, however formidable it may be, because sometimes philosophers and professors, when they are in front of a microphone, without notes, and are obliged to speak and to offer statements that otherwise they would qualify and complicate many times over if they had to write them and publish them—in such a situation, they find themselves *disarmed*, in a way, and they say things. And perhaps it is necessary, now, in a certain way, to be disarmed. Each one of us here has written texts on these questions: we are not going to "give an account" of them this evening. These texts are naturally better armed than our public speeches—at least that is the case for me. Nonetheless, I believe that in risking a way of speaking that is disarmed, there is something of a responsibility.

I do not want to hold the floor too long, we must let our speech circulate, that is the role of debate. Before going any further, however, before posing a few questions and risking a few hypotheses, I would like to put forth a request that is, at bottom, one that I have always implicitly put forth in France to those who have spoken on these grave problems or who have asked us to speak about them. I will suppose, then, that no one here is in any way favorable, or wishes to be favorable, to what we always very cursorily call Nazism, totalitarianism, fascism; and that we can establish as a protocol of discussion that no one is, in full awareness, to be suspected of wanting to defend those theses here. Also that no one claims to absolve Heidegger, to disculpate him or render him innocent of every kind of fault in that respect. This being admitted—that is in any case my hypothesis—, is it not possible, then, to be vigilant with regard to the discussions that develop on this subject (not only this evening but already for a long time, and in a more or less intense way for a few months), with regard to our discourse and our improvisations, in such a way that they would not contain or reproduce the gestures, the aggressions, the implications, the elements of scenography that recall *the very thing* against which we are allied?

Now, unfortunately, what has terrified me during the last few months is that, too often, the way the problems were posed, the way people were judged—I'm speaking of the living, not of Heidegger; I am speaking of those who read, who take a position and try to understand—the way things were staged and dramatized, with certain types of simplifications, conflations, analogisms, often recalled the worst for me: precisely that which they claimed to be opposing. I maintain that, in a field of problems of such gravity, every gesture that proceeds by conflation, precipitous totalization, short-circuited argumentation, simplification of statements, etc., is politically a very grave gesture that recalls—through formulas of denegation that would deserve the detour of an analysis in their own right—the very thing against which we are supposed to be working. I could give many examples; I will give only two. Since Professor Gadamer spoke a moment ago of logocentrism, I will take an example from the German press, and one from the French press—for it is there, is it not, that things have happened in recent months? Thus I read, in an article by M. van Rossum,[9] that the French Heideggerians, *all* of them, and in a way all of French thought, assembled into a block as a whole (there were a few names jumbled together), that this thought was, to the extent that it was interested only in Heidegger, totalitarian. This totalitarian gesture was meant to denounce totalitarianism. Then M. van Rossum went on to write that the word "logocentrism" was not invented in France but rather comes from Ludwig Klages,[10] and for the journalist this signified a contamination by the worst. It is exactly as if one said: careful, the word "concept" is found in Hegel. Personally, I didn't know that "logocentrism" came from Klages, but that would not have bothered me. For everyone knows very well that, in philosophy, a word is of no great importance as long as one has not constituted its function as a concept in a discourse. This is an example of anti-Nazi good conscience: I do not suspect the political choices of the author, but his professional gesture is, in my view, politically grave.

Likewise, in France, several times I have been accused—even though just recently I devoted a small book to Heidegger's Nazism and to what, it seems to me, may make it possible to begin to interpret a certain relationship between Heidegger's thought and Nazism—I am reproached for not denouncing Heidegger's Nazism! Whereas I speak of nothing else. As Philippe Lacoue-Labarthe said to me: what do they want? that you have printed in big letters on the cover of your book, "Fascism shall not pass"? So what I would wish, not only for this evening, but before and after, is that everyone remain vigilant in this regard. That in the discussion, and in the definition of responsibilities, the forms of trial and accusation not reproduce the very thing that is in question—and that, as we know, cannot be reduced to a period of German history, of the life of a party, of a regime, but that infiltrates and insinuates itself everywhere, and can do so again in the future. For these are questions of the future that we have to pose this evening. Political responsibility begins there—but does not end there.

I said when I began that we could perhaps ask about the signification of the encounter this evening. I do not know what will come of it; I said that I was afraid and perhaps that we are all expecting too much from it. But in any case, it is already very symbolic, before even beginning. The fact that in Germany, in Heidelberg, at your invitation, in your presence, with French people—the fact that the question of Heidegger's political thinking is being posed, this is already highly symbolic. Of what? Why is it, for example, that the spectacular and intense phase of this debate, which has lasted since 1933 and has known several different periods; how is it that the most public, most mediatic phase has occurred in France? For if we are here, this evening, among French and Germans, I think it is because of that.

The analysis always risks being insufficient for a phenomenon so rich; and if there were only one thread to follow, in order to understand what has happened in France in the course of these

last months, well, it would not have happened that way. If the phenomenon has been so irresistible, that is because it was *overdetermined*: one single cause could not explain its intensity. I certainly
cannot carry out the analysis of such an overdetermination; I
will only draw out a few threads, knowing very well that they are
insufficient. I would remark first that, very often, as seen from
Germany—from what I have read in the German press—, this debate remained very French . . . , and in a way that was not always
flattering. Thus one has said: the French became aware very late
of something that we, here, have known for a long time, and that
they would have known if they had not been so Heideggerian—if
Heideggerianism had not had the prosperity it has had in France
since the war, which it has not had in Germany.

I am not saying that this is false; I am saying that it is very
simplified and very reductive. First, there is not one single French
Heideggerianism, no more than there is one single legacy of Heidegger in France. I insist on this in order to detotalize the matter.
I believe that it is necessary to insist on the differences and the
ruptures that have marked the legacy of Heidegger. Since Professor
Gadamer wished to relate to us a few memories on this subject,
allow me briefly to do so as well. Often in Germany and in France
it is thought that the entire heritage of Heidegger was taken over
by [Jean] Beaufret and the friends of Beaufret. This is not true. For
my part—and I am speaking here of someone who was a student
after the war, from 1948 to 1951—, I knew nothing about Beaufret and became interested in Heidegger after reading Sartre and
Merleau-Ponty. Then, having begun to read Husserl and Heidegger
directly, I tried to free myself from both Sartre's and Merleau-
Ponty's readings of Heidegger and Husserl—and did so still without Beaufret. On the other hand, whatever one may say, and I will
certainly not be the last to do so, given certain negative effects
of Beaufret's capture of Heidegger's heritage (and as you know,
things are now taking a rather painful turn), I would also not want

to overlook the fact—and I feel all the freer to say this in that personally I have always been, for reasons that are not only political, very critical with regard to Beaufret's reading of Heidegger—, I would not want to overlook the fact that he did, at least, give to the letter of Heidegger an attention that did not consist merely of a rapid reappropriation, in the style of Sartre or Merleau-Ponty. He invited people to engage in a sort of faithful philology that, even if one did not agree, was not entirely negative.

Then over the course of the last twenty or twenty-five years, readings of Heidegger were developed—by Lacoue-Lacoue, by Jean-Luc Nancy, and I attempted one myself—that were neither Sartrian nor Merleau-Pontian, nor Beaufretian, and that, on the question of politics, were troubled very early on, as expressed through various turns of phrase and detours, but without leaving any doubt. These readings did not linger over external documents, which were available already since 1960–62; they tried to understand Heidegger's text itself: how this text, such a difficult text, could be articulated with what we know of the author's political engagements. This is not easy. It is not complete. We have made progress, but enormous work remains to be done.

Often, when I see so many people in France suddenly interested in Heidegger's Nazism, shouting loudly and accusing philosophers of having said nothing to them, and setting out to condemn not only Heidegger but also the living, I would like to ask them a very simple question: okay, let's talk; have you read *Sein und Zeit?* ... to take only that example. Those of us who began to read this book, to confront it in a close explication, in a questioning and nonorthodox way, know well that, among others, it is still waiting to be read; that there are still, in this text of Heidegger, immense resources. Consequently, one has a right to ask those who wish to draw very rapid conclusions linking the philosophical text and a political comportment that they begin at least to try to read. And I say this at the risk of appearing to defend Heidegger against accusations or condemnations: you know that that is not my intention in doing this.

If this affair exploded in France, on the occasion of Farias's book, and was then relayed by a certain number of other things, it is because, across the three veins, the three threads that I just drew out, Heidegger's questions, indeed, were present in the French philosophical field; and because they provoked tensions within it, virtual wars, so that there were some who at the first opportunity tried to exploit what Farias's "picture" might give them that could be immediately used against this or that French figure. This is far from being a total explanation: it is one element of an explanation.

Another element of an explanation would lead us back, I believe—and it seems to me that this evening it is necessary to insist on this, at the risk of neglecting other points—, [would bring us back] to the political situation in France and in Europe. At a moment when the destiny of Europe, as one says, is taking a certain path, when a certain political discourse dominates *the* discourse on politics in Europe, in France, in Germany, and in many other Western democracies, we see a confrontation between, on the one hand, a resurgence of ideologies and comportments that are not unrelated to what one identifies very quickly as Nazism, fascism, totalitarianism; and, on the other hand, a social-democratic discourse whose values of reference are those of the rights of man, of democracy, of the liberty of the subject. But that discourse is becoming conscious that it remains philosophically very fragile, that the strength of its consensus in official political discourses, or elsewhere, rests on very traditional philosophical axioms that often appear problematic, and in any case incapable of resisting what they are meant to oppose. Hence a certain disquiet, at this point even a certain fear, on the side of the tradition of this discourse—a fear regarding its own fragility and regarding a potential for questioning that is stronger in Heidegger's work than in many others, of course, and also, in any case, in the work of those who are interested in Heidegger's thought. Whatever reservations they may have, and whatever their different critiques of him may be, there are people who are interested in this potential for questioning that one finds in Heidegger, and so the forms of these questions become very threatening. All the more in that, very often—I think this is the case for those who are here this evening, for the French in particular—it is not very easy to accuse them, these people, of being, even a little, on the Right. Well, what is happening? Whence the nervousness, the fear, and the compulsion to accuse very quickly, to judge, to simplify? It is this compulsion that seems to me to be extremely grave as a symptom.

I cannot enter into detail this evening (perhaps we will do so when the time comes for questions, if this debate continues) concerning the content of these complicated relations to Heidegger that have been maintained by certain French people—among whom are some here this evening. These relations are in any case unlike those of Sartre or Merleau-Ponty, or of Beaufret. But I would like to say a word now about Germany, because I find here, too, that the accusations I have heard launched against the way in which a certain heritage of Heidegger was established in France, or by which one would have let oneself be blinded, for a long time, concerning Heidegger's Nazi engagement, I find these accusations to be very unjust. I asked myself why these accusations, too, were so compulsive, so precipitous and globalizing; why analogism and conflation were so often practiced in Germany around this question. My hypotheses are numerous; there are at least two.

One is that for well-known historical reasons, the relation to Heidegger became so intolerable that, aside from a few exceptions, naturally, Heidegger has been little read in Germany since the war. Consequently, one bypassed what some in France, also for historical reasons, had the freedom to read, having less of a bad conscience in approaching Heidegger. One bypassed a certain reading of Heidegger. I do not wish, in turn, to simplify unjustly: I know that Heidegger was read by some, well read, and still is. Nonetheless, at the macroscopic level where I must remain now, one must indeed say that the reading of Heidegger in Germany was rather repressed since the war. That is a first hypothesis.

Next, this repression was bound to produce, in the form of a projection-expulsion, a desire to accuse, from the other side of the border, those who for their part had anything to do with Heidegger. And these are the symptoms I evoked a moment ago.

So I think that what is symbolized by an encounter like the one this evening, whatever its results, or the disappointment that would have to follow from it, [what is symbolized] is the possibility, today, thanks to these provocations, of lifting the inhibitions on every side, and of not only reading Heidegger with the political vigilance required, but of *reading* him. I believe that those who in France, very quickly, from the first week following the appearance of Farias's book, said, Heidegger is finished, no need to read him any more—they would almost have said, Let's burn him!—, such people demonstrated not only their terrifying political irresponsibility (with the good conscience, naturally, of their unwavering anti-Nazism), but also of their sociological inexperience. For it is evident that Heidegger is going to become more and more interesting: it is up to us to act in such a way that, in reading as rigorously as possible, and in as responsible a way as possible, Heidegger's text, his *entire* text—the rectoral address, the political speeches, but also all the other texts—, [to act in such a way that] we not renounce the political responsibility that must be ours; and that we define a political responsibility that takes account of Heidegger's questions.

I have, for my part—but I said that I didn't want to "give an account" of published texts—I have been interested by what, in Heidegger, on the one hand, made it possible to question the traditional categories of responsibility, of the subject, for example, of right [*du droit*], and what let itself nonetheless, up to a certain point, be limited by this questioning—and even, perhaps, by the form of the question.

Without wanting to use grand words or to give in to diplomatic convention and say that "the destiny of Europe is at stake," I do believe that it is the question of Europe that brings us together here. And I believe that this responsibility with regard to Europe calls for a redefinition of responsibility: not an evasion but a redefinition. For in my opinion, the discourse that dominates European institutions is no longer capable of *holding up*, and those who put forth this discourse know this in an obscure way. You know that one of the violences to which the people who pose this kind of question are exposed—and this happens to us, it has happened to Lacoue-Labarthe, it happens to me—, is that when one says that ethics, that the way we define ethics today is shaking on its lack of foundation, or when we say that we no longer know very well what it means to be responsible, the violence to which we are exposed is that one says to us: so you are putting forth a discourse that is immoral, an irresponsible discourse!

I maintain, on the contrary, that deconstruction today, for example, which was evoked by Professor Gadamer, even when it places in question this axiomatic of subjectivity or of responsibility, or when it places in question certain axioms of Heidegger's discourse, is of course not an abdication of responsibility; it is, in my view in any case, the most difficult responsibility that I can take. And to trust in traditional categories of responsibility seems to me today to be, precisely, irresponsible.

I believe therefore that, whatever vertiginous confusion might arise for us in the absence of certainty regarding these new responsibilities, this must not for all that push us to take refuge, to rush toward the old discourses. In this respect, we know well that these old discourses are not exempt from complicities, with Nazism, for example—I could say totalitarianism, fascism, Stalinism, things that must not be confounded among themselves, but that, for a moment, we will place together. The complicities between a discourse that is, let's say, humanist and democratic but that has not reelaborated in a critical fashion its own categories, and that which it is meant to oppose—these complicities are always possible, are they not? And our vigilance is there and must be there. But I have already spoken too long, I will stop here.

RW: Thank you very much, Monsieur Derrida. You are aware how important your point of view is for us, and not only concerning Victor Farias's publication—it is quite evident that, for you, it is not a matter of judging the quality of a book but of finding in it a provocation for thinking responsibility. Because for us Germans this question of responsibility is also crucial. Moreover, I find particularly interesting that you have broadened the scope of the very specific discussion that you had previously with Professor Gadamer, on the question of logocentrism. But before coming back to these points, I turn now to M. Lacoue-Labarthe.

PHILIPPE LACOUE-LABARTHE: Although I am the fourth to speak, I would like to repeat, but not simply for the sake of form, the words of thanks and gratitude that I share, and that I feel I owe to you first of all, and to Mireille Calle-Gruber, whom I would like to thank deeply for having initiated this encounter. At the same time, I would like to indicate very briefly that, for me in any case, not only am I afraid, as Jacques Derrida has said, but my presence here, on this subject, is something that I find very imposing. Not because of the location, but because for someone of my generation (I was born in 1940), to come here to speak, in my language, before a German public, on the subject of the drama, and even of the catastrophe that Germany went through in the years when I was beginning my life, all this is very imposing. Finally, a third preliminary precaution: I will nonetheless try to be brief, otherwise I fear that there may not be a debate, properly speaking. And obviously, given our position, Jacques Derrida and myself, I too will take my point of departure from the French scene. I said that I am from the generation of 1940. For this simple reason, I do not therefore have quite the same perception of that scene and of what is involved in it as Derrida. This is the case, essentially, on two points. The first is that this question, the question of Nazism, of fascism, of the totalitarianisms, if you will, is as it were a family question. What I mean by this is that I feel implicated and concerned by this question, taking "family" in a broad sense, of course. Because in France there was Vichy, because, as for all French people of my generation (I was five, six, seven years old), one began to teach me the epic, almost, of the Resistance, while remaining silent on what had happened during the four or five years before 1945. I gradually discovered, very simply, that France had been implicated in this affair, well beyond even what I could have thought. And in particular, implicated in anti-Semitism; and if not directly in the massacre or the extermination, in any case in the deportation, in the delivery, if I dare say, of the Jews to Germany.

This is still a family affair because, in the discourse, the language, the statements that suffused my childhood and my adolescence, in high school and in my surroundings, I heard pass a countless number of anti-Semitic phrases pronounced by schoolmates and friends, by adults, who were not particularly extreme right wing, but for whom this language was more or less natural. And for a long time, that is to say since I entered the profession of philosophy, it has been clear to me that this is a question that I had to take on, and that there was something there that was more than grave, in my view. And that, in a certain way, I had to work out a certain relationship, not so much with those in my entourage as with what, as a French person, I would have therefore been since my childhood, in my possibility.

What would I have been, if I had been twenty years old in 1935 or in 1940? What would I have thought? What would I have done? On what side would I have placed myself? According to the contingencies of my upbringing and education, of my family (this time in the restricted sense)? Or in a word, according to this multiple "causality," if you will, which remains all the same a causality in the trajectory or in the movement of an existence. I believe that, when one touches on these problems, this is a question that one should never forget to ask oneself. What would I have done, given that it was only *afterward* that I gradually discovered all this?

The second reason why I no doubt do not perceive the French scene in quite the same way, nor in the same terms— although I absolutely agree with what Jacques Derrida has said and in particular with regard to the reading of Heidegger (in this respect we are exposed to virtually the same criticisms)—, the [second] reason is that, in philosophy, the generation of 1940 signifies something in particular in France. There is a generation of the war that, at bottom, came into the philosophical profession after the generation of 1930 and that was in large part formed by this preceding generation. I was, for example, the student of Gérard Granel, and it was when I was a student that I read the first texts of Jacques Derrida. That is one reason—a question of age or a lack of precociousness, if you like—why I was not involved in the elaboration of what two French journalists call "la pensée 68" (the thought of 68).[11] And my perception of the Farias affair today is that it is not at all a matter of a concerted operation, no; it is rather that Farias was perceived with a sort of relief. Not only as the un-expected opportunity finally to be able to breathe, by getting rid of Heidegger, his insurmountable difficulty, the radicality of his questions, etc.; Farias also provided an opportunity to sanction the negative verdict, to say the least, that had been handed down against the so-called thought of 68. In other words: since this "pensée 68" was purportedly entirely dominated by Heidegger, if not totally servile to Heidegger, well, then, since we had a Nazi Heidegger (from one end to the other, from the age of fourteen to eighty), we could now get rid of, or more exactly sanction, the all-out attack on this "pensée 68." And the stakes are there—for me in any case. I see emerging, against the background of an extreme simplification of the problems, also against the background of a real animosity, and of a kind of philosophical return, I would even say a philosophical regression—I see emerging an attack, which

Farias, or at least his so-called conclusions, will help to authorize, to legitimize. This attack aims quite simply to restore a certain number of things.

It must not be forgotten that among those who are attempting to construct, in a way that is quite fragile (here too I share Derrida's opinion), a kind of liberal philosophy, social-democratic, if you like, founded on what one of the two journalists I mentioned a moment ago calls a "juridical humanism," it must not be forgotten that among those who are involved in this operation, now certified by what the media have named the "new philosophy"—and it was Christian Jambet who wrote the preface to Farias's book in France—, there are a good number of former Stalinists or ultra-Stalinists who supported in their time, and more or less during the period when we were students together, a number of political movements whose inanity I for my part saw before '68, and even more so after. It is more or less the same people who found their way to constructing, to an attempt to construct this "juridical humanism"; and it is the same people who, in order to construct that humanism, are in the process of finding authorization in Farias's denunciation, for the purposes of attacking what is nonetheless the most forceful and most powerful work that French thought has produced since the war—that is, this so-called "pensée 68." There is in this an undeniably political scene being played out. And I believe that this must not be passed over in silence.

I will add as well, on this point, that this is the reason why I do not at all believe, despite the enormous and very intense media effects of this affair, I do not believe that the debate is, as Baudrillard indicated some time ago in a French newspaper, of the order of the simulacrum. I do not believe at all that it is too late to pose these questions or to comprehend what they are about. I do not at all believe that it was only at the time that we would have found the only language that would be adequate and that would make it possible to deal with it. It seems to me, on the contrary, that it is

perhaps only today that we are capable of beginning an attempt
at an analysis of Nazism, of the fascisms; because it is in effect
the first time that, on the one hand, we are at bottom rid of the
communist . . . obstacle, let's call it (I'm speaking of the French
situation), or the para-communist obstacle, that is, the Marxist obstacle—the way in which sometimes, in France, one "gets rid" of an
ideology is not something I approve; at times it is quite strange—,
and on the other hand, because we are perhaps capable of initiat-
ing an analysis of Nazism precisely for having read Heidegger. I
know that this may sound like a pure paradox, but, for me at least,
it is the reading of Heidegger that, I believe—provided that one
carry it out in a certain way, of course—can give access to a certain
reality of Nazism. An access that the univocal moral and political
accusation—which of course I share; but in fact when one tries
to carry out philosophical work one cannot after all limit oneself
to that—has continued to mask. I will even add that the strictly
political accusation (and the way in which the signifier *fascist* has
functioned for people of my generation is a symptom of this), the
political accusation of Nazism as the incarnation of *the* political
evil simply forbids this access.

From the moment when one began to distrust the use of the
word "fascist," from the moment when there was a questioning of
what is called leftist totalitarianism, from that moment, perhaps, it
is possible for real work to begin. And that is the reason why—this
is one of my grievances against Farias's book—the simplification
that consists in presenting Heidegger as entirely Nazi seems to me
extremely unfortunate in this story: because perhaps it will be necessary, for a certain time still, to fight about this presentation, in
order to try to make it understood that, in Heidegger, one of the
secrets of Nazism has remained unperceived up to now.

(After a break, the session is resumed.)

RW: It is somewhat difficult to get the discussion going after
these major statements by our guests. It is perhaps useful to recall

that the philosophers present here—Lacoue-Labarthe prefers
"thinkers" to "philosophers"—, let us say then that the thinkers
present here were inspired by Heidegger in their work, but in
very different ways. It seems to me that the moment has come to
stress these differences. Beginning with the overview that was just
offered to us, I will propose, if you will permit me, to emphasize a
first question that could be discussed: that of logocentrism. For in
Derrida's conception, the critique of European philosophy and the
philosophy of Heidegger proceed from this perspective. Derrida
puts forth the thesis that all European philosophy finds itself, in
a certain way, corrupted by logocentrism. Professor Gadamer, in
his statement, cast doubt on this hypothesis, not only concerning Heidegger, but also the entire European philosophical tradition. This evening, I have the impression that M. Derrida's use of
the word "logocentrism" is much broader than at the time of the
discussion that took place in Paris. At that time, logocentrism was
very narrowly linked to phonocentrism, whereas today you are
using it in the sense of a categorical *avoir raison*," of a terrible
simplification.

JD: The practical problem that we face is the following: for
the debate to take place, it is necessary that we not speak too long;
but with these difficult problems, it is hardly possible to explain
oneself with any seriousness without speaking for a long time.
So . . . I will try to do both at the same time!

I will lay out a few preliminaries before speaking of logocentrism, for you have said that in France many thinkers, many philosophers, if not all, were inspired by Heidegger. That, I believe, is
not false, but it needs to be qualified. I believe that in France, with
the exception perhaps of Beaufret and of certain of his students,
all those who were "inspired," as you said, by Heidegger, and not
inspired in the sense only of being in the school of Heidegger, but
who became interested in him—for there have been no Heideggerians in France and not only because, as Philippe Lacoue-Labarthe

recalled, being a Heideggerian had no meaning—, all those, then, who were marked by their reading of Heidegger have had a polemical relation with him, in the most noble sense of this word: it was an *Auseinandersetzung* [a critical "explication"] for them all. And in a very different way in each case.

There is one thing that struck me: I think of someone like Foucault, for example (or Deleuze), who—in contrast to those who like myself *declared* their interest in Heidegger and wrote on him—practically never cited or named Heidegger, and who declared, some time before his death, that his reading of Heidegger had been decisive. What does this mean? During twenty-five years of production, of publication, of work, to have such an *undeclared* relation to Heidegger—a legible relation, after all, for those who read both Foucault and Heidegger. How to explain that the book Deleuze has just devoted to Foucault ends with declarations of the type: an explication is necessary between Foucault and Heidegger, that is where everything happens, etc., etc., whereas Deleuze never mentions Heidegger by name (except once or twice in a book on Nietzsche). Thus there was here a very powerful relationship to Heidegger, albeit one that was denied.

For others, like Levinas, the relation to Heidegger is evident, declared, also polemical, very deep. For Blanchot, for Jean-Luc Nancy, for Lacoue-Labarthe, it is evident. As for myself, and since you asked me to say a word about this, I have always been . . . very shocked (since we are speaking in such tones this evening, let us do so), very shocked by certain commentaries, certain "readings" (let's not be too polemical) that presented me as Heideggerian—with a difference in style, it is said—whereas I am completely conscious, and I am not saying this because now there has been Farias and a few others, I am completely conscious, since the beginning of my reading and my references to Heidegger, of having been in an "explication" with him that has always and only been very *troubled*. I could give many examples of this, beginning with this little book *Of Spirit*.[12] Since always, and more and more, I have been at once convinced of the force and the necessity of Heidegger's questions, while at the same time I see, I won't say their insufficiency, but something in them that called—and I believe that it is being very faithful to Heidegger to say this—not only for progress in questioning, but for another type of questioning, a possible counter-questioning, and possible . . . questions about the question, that is, about the privileges that the question still maintained in Heidegger even up to his last texts; texts, notably, like those of *Unterwegs zur Sprache*,[13] where thinking was defined as "questioning."[14] We can come back to this. But I have tried precisely to demarcate how, in this text, Heidegger's trajectory beginning from the unquestioned privilege of the question all the way to a reorientation in another text of *Unterwegs zur Sprache* could have, at a certain moment, a relation with the political matters of which we are speaking here.[15]

Consequently, I have had the feeling—and I believe that this is true for all the French who have been rapidly categorized as Heideggerian—of having this polemical relationship to Heidegger. And in a way that is much freer than one has been able to do in Germany, for the political reasons I spoke of a moment ago. I have never felt, for biographical reasons that it would be easy for me to explain—but that there is no need for me to go into this evening—, [I have never been] suspected of sympathy for anything connected with the Right, with anything Nazi, etc. Therefore, very freely, one reads Heidegger: one has no shame in reading him.

Logocentrism. I will make two distinctions (one is obliged to operate massively in such a situation). I will distinguish, first, logocentrism from phonocentrism. Phonocentrism is not a philosophy, it is a structural situation that pushes humanity, and not only European humanity, under certain conditions, in certain phases of its evolution, to privilege the voice. This is not only Greco-European. There is phonocentrism everywhere. It is not an evil. I would therefore not speak of corruption: I have always been rather mistrustful with regard to those who speak of corruption—in any domain. Phonocentrism is therefore an irreducible structure in the economy of human culture. . . . Fine, but it would be necessary immediately to correct all these words, for here it is not only a question of the "human": it is *Dasein*; and not only *Dasein*, but perhaps something else again. . . . Let's say: an irreducible structure. Logocentrism is not universal, as phonocentrism is. Logocentrism is, indeed, something Greco-European, which one also cannot globalize, totalize. I do not believe that one can speak of *the* logocentrism, of *the* logocentric metaphysics, even if it has happened here or there that I have yielded to imprudent formulations. But there is a logocentric structure that amounts to a privileging of logos. This also means many things. . . . When I utilized this term, which I didn't know that Ludwig Klages had used, I did so in a very particular French situation, at the moment when the hegemony of linguistic structuralism was in full swing, when everything was language, when everything had to be understood in terms of linguistic structures, and when, on the other hand, in Heidegger too there was a certain logocentrism.

However, my readings of Heidegger in this respect have always been very complicated: I believe that there was something of a logocentrism in Heidegger, but there was also something else, much more complex. Logos and phonocentrism represent in Heidegger something that *is at work* [*est à l'oeuvre*], even if it cannot be reduced to something that is globalizable. There is a privileging of presence (I am saying this in a very massive way). And from the beginning, from that point of view, I believe that the questions that I asked about Heidegger were also political questions, were they not? I believe this was marked quite clearly, even if it was not in the code in which this is done today. I assert as well, nonetheless, that the questioning of this phonocentrism and of this logocentrism, in all the dimensions in which such a questioning was susceptible of being oriented, also could not do without certain Heideggerian resources. The difficult strategy was therefore

precisely to have recourse to certain Heideggerian gestures, up to
a certain point, in order potentially if not to resolve them, at least
to bend them, to turn them back on themselves and to analyze
what might constitute certain limits in Heidegger's text.

I do not wish to speak for too long, but . . . since I am speaking now I would like to say something else, in response to, or as
an echo or an extension of what Philippe Lacoue-Labarthe said a
moment ago. I am going to say here, at bottom, something very
serious, which I have never said—since I make it a rule for myself
never to recount published texts. What then is this thing about
which everyone is in agreement? For I believe that most of us
are in agreement on the fact that, even if one could understand,
explain, excuse the engagement of 1933 and some of the consequences that came after, in a complicated and equivocal manner,
the years that followed, what is *unforgivable* (this is Lacoue-
Labarthe's word), what is "a wound for thought," as Blanchot
says, is the silence after the war, on Auschwitz, etc. Well, according
to the protocol that I laid out a moment ago, I share, I have the
feeling of this wound, I can think like Lacoue-Labarthe, Blanchot,
and some others on this question. But I wonder what would have
happened if Heidegger had said something—and what he could
have said.

What I am saying here is very risky, and I risk it as a hypothesis, while asking you to accompany me in this risk. Suppose that
Heidegger had said not only, "it was a tremendous *Dummheit*, a
stupid thing, a *bêtise*, in 1933," but: "Auschwitz is the absolute horror" (which it is, is it not?), "it is the thing that we must condemn,
that I radically condemn. . . ." Fine. These are phrases that all of
us say. At that moment, what would have happened? He would
probably have been absolved, more easily absolved. One might
have closed the file on the relations between Heidegger's thought
and the event called Nazism, the overdetermined events called
Nazism; with a phrase spoken in the direction of an easy consensus, Heidegger would have *closed* the matter. And we would not

today be in the process of asking ourselves—as we *must* do—what Heidegger's experience of thought could have in the way of affinities, synchrony, common roots with this still unthought thing that Nazism is for us. I believe that if he had let himself go for a statement, let's say, of immediate moral reaction, or of a declaration of horror, or of non-forgiveness—a declaration that would not itself be a work of thought at the level of all that he had already thought—, well, perhaps we would feel more easily spared the work that we have to do today: because *we* have to do this work. That is what we have inherited. And I consider that the terrifying, perhaps unforgivable, silence of Heidegger, the absence of phrases like those we want to hear, of those that we are capable of pronouncing on the subject of Nazism, or on his relation to Nazism, that absence leaves us with an inheritance, leaves us with the *injunction* to think what he did not think. I believe indeed—this was said by Lacoue-Labarthe in particular—that there is something of Nazism that Heidegger *did not think*. At least he did not pretend, as it would have been easy to do, to have understood what had happened and to condemn it. I believe that, perhaps, Heidegger said to himself: I will only be able to pronounce a condemnation of Nazism if I can pronounce it in a language that would not only measure up to what I have already said, but also to what happened there. And that; he was not capable of that. And this silence is perhaps an honest way of recognizing that he was not capable of that. That is a very risky hypothesis: I said that I was improvising it this evening.

Without this silence, without this *terrible* silence, we would not feel the injunction placed on our responsibility before the necessity of reading Heidegger as he did not read himself—at least he didn't claim to. Or perhaps he did claim to, and it is there I suppose that he thus comforted himself in his silence, that he had already said, in his way, without giving in to easy statements, what, in Nazism, was bound to be corrupted—to take up your term, M. Wiehl. That whoever wanted to find in his texts something with

which to condemn not the inner truth of this great movement,
but its degradation or its perdition, well, one could find it there.
And that he did not have to say anything more about it. That he
was not *able* to say more about it. He was not able to say anything more. So it is up to us, if we want to do more than say: yes,
Auschwitz, it is the absolute horror, one of the absolute horrors
of human history; if we can do more, it is up to us to do it. And I
believe that this injunction, it is inscribed in what is most terrifying
but perhaps also most valuable as a chance in the heritage left by
Heidegger. I believe, and here I agree with Lacoue-Labarthe, that
the reading of Heidegger can help us, not on its own, of course,
and not a simply orthodox and philological reading, but a certain
active reading of Heidegger can help us to approach a way to think
through what we condemn.

   RW: Monsieur Lacoue-Labarthe, I am going to ask you to
speak, since you have worked a great deal on this unthought of
Heidegger.

   PL-L: I will try to do so, at least, since . . . I have the same
difficulty as Jacques Derrida: this is difficult to say in a few words.
   A moment ago, indeed, I asserted that the secret of Nazism,
in a certain way, was in Heidegger—a phrase that is obviously hasty
and much too simple. But one can try, for a moment, to follow
this thread. I agree with what Jacques Derrida just said: there is
something that Heidegger did not claim to think. Though on one
point I would make this remark: Heidegger, on occasion, could be
capable of phrases that are simply moral, phrases of great simplicity, all things considered; Heidegger pronounced these phrases.
But I completely agree that if he had said, "Auschwitz is the absolute horror," at bottom, he would have been absolved without
much effort.
   However, he did after all make certain declarations after the
war, on multiple occasions, in which he did no more than deplore
the fate of German prisoners in the east—and he did it with great

simplicity, in fact, saying, let us remember. Let us remember because memory, *Andenken*, is thought, *Denken*. There is then after
all a difference in treatment, dare I say, that, personally, continues and will continue to shock me. That said, with regard to the
matter of thinking, as he would have said, I am persuaded indeed
that Heidegger left behind texts in which, if one knows how to
read them, and to read them perhaps against his own reading, the
reading that he himself would have given, there are in any case
elements that could lead one to search for an interpretation
of Nazism.

I will briefly explain what I mean. I believe first of all that,
contrary to what Farias has said, there is more than a rupture—
we have to do with a movement that is much more complex than
a rupture—, there is a very profound and almost devastating
movement that affects Heidegger's thought in the years 1935–40,
perhaps longer. We do not have all the texts, all the courses, all
the teaching concerning which Heidegger indicated more than
once that they had a certain relation to what he himself called the
Kehre [the "turn"]; and in this movement that affects Heidegger's
thought, one can recognize with a certain obviousness an effect of
his political adventure. And even if one can multiply the anecdotes
to show that he maintained a relationship with the hierarchy of
the regime, or the university authorities enrolled in the party, it
is of course the movement of his thought that must make demands on us.

This movement forced him in a certain way, and as everyone
knows, to open up problematics that he had not taken on before
then. For example, the question of *Dichtung*, the reading of
Hölderlin; for example, the reading, both critical and deconstructive, of Nietzsche; for example, the problematic of freedom with
the reading of Schelling's treatise; and here, in these texts, internal to these texts, I believe that he engaged in an immense debate
with Nazism. Not Nazism in its strictly political reality—to be sure,
there are phrases in Heidegger directed against this or that person,

against the ideologizing use of Nietzsche, for which Nietzsche
would be partly responsible, and this is very clear and readable on
the surface of the text—, but an immense debate on what National
Socialism is, one could say, in the history of the West; on how it
is the end result, in a certain way, of this history, and on its secret
essence. It is for that reason alone that I spoke of a secret: it seems
to me, and I too do not want to recount what there is in my book
(I find that useless and impossible), it seems to me that it is when
he enters into the question of art, and when he calls aesthetics
into question—and you know that he considers "aesthetics" to be
the philosophy of art since Plato and Aristotle, even though he
knows very well that it is a discipline that emerged quite late—,
when he undertakes to deconstruct Western aesthetics, it seems to
me that it is partly there (I am not saying that this is the only place
where the secret for Heidegger is harbored, is hidden) that his debate with National Socialism is to be found. Because it is there, of
course, that we find the question, which for him was so complex,
of the essence of *technê*; because it is there that he carries on a
debate with himself, between, at bottom, a Jüngerian version, from
that time, of technics in the *Gestalt* of the worker, and another
interpretation that, I believe, he glimpses, and that perhaps he will
begin to arrive at much later, in the 1950s, precisely when he will
be capable of *delimiting* Jünger's position; because it is there too
that he grapples with what one could call, too quickly (and I ask
you to forgive me for that), his own Nietzscheanism, his way of
being and above all of having been Nietzschean, in a certain manner, at the very beginning of the 1930s. (Of course it would take
some time to show this.) And because it is there, too, but likewise
in terms of freedom, that he engages a debate with what is called
German idealism—that is, with speculative idealism.

From the moment when Heidegger's engagement (to describe it roughly) proceeded from the idea that Germany, because
of speculative idealism, or because of philosophy between Leibniz

and Nietzsche, held in itself the entire intellectual or even spiritual heritage of the West—and from the moment when Heidegger did this just as all the great Germans of the tradition had done, every one of them without exception (and I am not excluding Marx), one arrives at the observation that Germany had no real historical existence—, then, I believe, one can comprehend Heidegger's gesture in favor of National Socialism. I imagine his very profound belief in the possibility of a radical National-Socialist revolution. This is a gesture that can be explained in terms of the hope of seeing Germany, in revealing itself capable of fulfilling its philosophical destiny, become something like the last figure of the West, and precisely thereby to acquire finally something like its identity; or to regain finally, if I think of this terminology, something like its proper being.

If this is what Heidegger thought in 1933—and for my part I am persuaded that this is what he was thinking—, then it throws a completely different light not on what Nazism was in its reality (although I do not much like this distinction), but in any case on what it could have represented with regard to thought, and finally, on what in a certain manner it could be potentially in its possibility. If Heidegger emphasized, in his rectoral address, the motif of *Führung*, which would require an endless amount of time to analyze in all its complexity, it is at least for this reason that he judged that a certain direction—which at that time he called "spiritual"—of the movement could perhaps enable the said movement to accede to the truth that he, Heidegger, believed he glimpsed.

Consequently, if it is at this depth that Heidegger at one and the same time tried to think and in a certain manner had the experience with National Socialism, then I am persuaded that a reading of Heidegger—which, I hasten to say, I have barely sketched on this point—is perhaps one of the paths, as he would have said, that will give us access to this thing that is National Socialism, which I believe to be still deeply unthought.

RW: Thank you. I find it essential for our discussion that you have emphasized that it is a question not only of a "stupidity" on Heidegger's part between 1933 and 1934, but that there are deeper reasons, which you have found in a tradition, in a certain aestheticism, in a Nietzschean reading. And on the other hand, I want to emphasize the problem that M. Derrida presented to us earlier, according to which there exist certain relations between Heidegger's logocentrism and something that he did not think and that is perhaps a basis for his National-Socialist engagement.

HG-G: We are all very tired, I think, and for me it remains still very difficult to be sure that I have really understood.

My intervention has two main points: on the one hand, there is logocentrism. This is a point on which I would like to articulate the convergence, the affinity between your own ideas and those that I and others have developed in the same perspective. But on the other hand, there is the problem of politics. I too see it as the real problem in which are located the reasons for Heidegger's renunciation of this rather simple solution that consisted in saying, "Ah, that was something shameful." I am impressed by your hypothesis (I hope I understand correctly) that it would have been too easy. And in any case, it is true, the inheritance left to us by his silence appears to me more fertile than a response he would have given, perhaps with a good conscience, but also by setting up the disproportion between the gravity of the event and the solution of such a response.

In my view, Heidegger, I believe, was a true visionary: with regard to the future in which so many problems are inscribed, concerning the last man, with regard to Nietzsche, to the forgetting of being; and your critique, my dear colleague Lacoue-Labarthe, concerning the text where Heidegger speaks of the industrial production of death, is in the line of this vision. This perspective so preoccupied him that even this extreme shame for our nation, the extermination of the Jews, even that appeared to him as something minimal compared to the future that awaits us.

In another respect, when I read "Ousia and Gramme," the first great essay, almost a book, reproduced in *Margins*,[16] I saw immediately this affinity with Heidegger's torment: there is no language to say the problem of being [*le problème de l'être*], which, with the article, is already a falsification.[17] How to approach this? How to think with this vision? In that sense, I believe that your description of the trace of the trace is quite close to all the things that Heidegger had in mind when he spoke of this deficiency of language.

As for me . . . I ask you to forgive me, each one has his own point of view, and mine here is inscribed against Heidegger. I say, certainly, Heidegger tried to arrive at a fragmentation of metaphysical conceptualization by means of this force that he exerted against words—*Was heisst Denken?*—, this in order to arrive at something that commands one to think. And you proceed, for your part, in a similar way. I see very well that there is also, on this point, something of a problem having to do with Paul Celan; but I am, all the same, the ally of Celan in this case, for with him fragmentation finds itself reinserted into the poem, into the song. As for me, therefore, as for my own more modest claim, I would say . . . that it is in *conversation* that I am searching.

JD: I sense that it is necessary for me to take up the thread with "conversation." . . . At the time of our meeting in Paris, a few years ago, that was already the question. And the conversation continues, as you see. . . .

H-GG: Ah! Each one thinks one thing, as Heidegger said. . . .

JD: I have nothing against conversation. I believe that it supposes this interruption of which you spoke before. And already, the last time, in Paris, the question was to know how to think the interruption, without which there is no relation to the other . . .

H-GG: Certainly.

JD: . . . and therefore no conversation. And this rupture—I am picking up on what you were saying, am I not, I am always picking up the thread . . .

H-GG: Yes indeed.

JD: . . . I am in the conversation—there are several ways to think the rupture in the relation to the other, a rupture that is the condition of the relation to the other, its very structure. And I recall that the question of psychoanalysis had arisen at that moment, between us. It was a question of knowing whether a hermeneutics like yours (I am summarizing very roughly) would be able to integrate psychoanalysis . . .

H-GG: But certainly.

JD: . . . or whether what psychoanalysis introduces as rupture, or as interruption, yes . . .

H-GG: But always within the exchange, naturally.

JD: . . . should not oblige any hermeneutics, or any thought of interpretation, to restructure itself entirely. And here, I return to our subject: Heidegger. For what I have tried to do with Heidegger, perhaps since a long time ago, but in a more explicit way more recently (for example, in the little book *Of Spirit*), is to read Heidegger not only beyond or independently from his own meaning-to-say [*vouloir-dire*], but even beyond what a certain psychoanalysis, with its conceptual apparatus and its axiomatics, was able to give us as an instrument: repression, denegation, displacement, etc. For example, let's follow as a thread the motif of *avoidance* in Heidegger: what does "avoiding" mean, for him? He said it in the beginning: it is necessary to avoid, *vermeiden*, the word "spirit"; but then he did not avoid it. In asking myself therefore what "avoiding" means in that case, I thought that it was necessary neither to trust in a familiar concept of avoidance nor, much less, in a psychoanalytic concept of avoidance, of denegation, because this psychoanalytic concept was, in my opinion, too weak, or incapable of sustaining the Heideggerian questioning itself.

It was necessary therefore to think something of avoidance, of denegation in particular, in the relation to politics, which for the moment could not be comprehensible, categorizable, with anything that is available in the current field of our interpretation. That is what interested me: how to think avoidance in Heidegger, in particular in politics.

When, for example, Heidegger tells us, not only concerning the word "spirit," about which he writes in *Sein und Zeit* that it must be avoided, but then he reintroduces it with quotation marks, in *Sein und Zeit* already, and then reintroduces it later *without* quotation marks—when he tells us, in 1951, responding, I think, to students in Zurich: "If I had to write a theology"—and I know, Professor Gadamer, that you have been interested in the religious dimension of Heidegger's thought—, "If I had to write a theology, which I sometimes dream of doing, the word 'being' would never appear in it,"—what does this mean? What does it mean that someone dares to say this, in 1951, after an immense trajectory marked by a tireless questioning of being? He did not write this; he said it, and Beda Alleman wrote it down. But it happens that the word "being" itself, at a given moment, in *Zur Seinsfrage*, Heidegger began to cross it out, with a *kreuzweise Durchstreichung*, mistrusting, precisely, an objectivizing representation of being, and specifying that this *Durchstreichung* in the form of a cross had nothing negative about it.[18] That it was necessary to think it in its relation to the *Geviert* [the "fourfold"], on the one hand, and, on the other, on the basis of this site that is at the center of the crossing through and of the *Geviert*.[19] It is not a negative sign there.

This means that he has always thought—since he says then that he should have always made this gesture of crossing out—that it was necessary to avoid the word "being," to avoid writing it in this way. Therefore, in a certain way he always did what he said he would have had to do if he wrote a theology. . . . But these modes of avoidance or of denegation cannot be apprehended, dominated, with the current familiar concepts of avoidance, because these current concepts, whether they pertain to the language of everyday life or to psychoanalytic conceptuality, they have not yet been put to the test of Heidegger's questioning concerning the history of ontology, concerning negation. . . . It is necessary, therefore, already, in order to decipher Heidegger's denegation, Heidegger's avoidance, to construct concepts . . . or let's say, modes of reading what is written in Heidegger—not only what he says but of his manner of writing. Modes of reading that are unknown and that in any case Heidegger himself did not produce, or was not able to produce.

Personally, this is what interests me, and I do not know if it can be placed within a hermeneutics; I do not know if the concept of interpretation or of hermeneutics is the relevant concept for designating this type of operation.

H-GG: Let us set hermeneutics aside. I believe that we are at the beginning of a conversation, and I thank you very much. It is beginning now.

JD: It is beginning.

H-GG: But what is beginning? The reconstruction of a text, of fragments, as psychoanalysis does, and as we must do if we want to survive.

JD: Yes. . . . I would not necessarily say psychoanalysis. But if what you call conversation must continue—which I hope for, for as long as possible—, it is necessary, so that this conversation be truly open in the relation to the other and in what it supposes in terms of interruption, alterity, yes . . .

H-GG: I agree completely.

JD: . . . then it is necessary to take responsibility for that which, of the future, remains still undecided.

H-GG: I agree with that.

JD: That is why, for me, conversation, if there is one—I don't know if I would use that word to say this, but let us take this word that is yours—, supposes that risk, the greatest risk, in a certain way.

RW: There remain more questions than there are responses to be given to them, but that is normal . . . according to hermeneutics. Perhaps we could, if you are not too tired, open the discussion to the public? For those who wish to intervene in German, a translation will be made.

(As an aside, Hilde Domin asks a question in German, to which Gadamer responds.)[20]

H-GG: I will first try to repeat what I understood of the question from Mme Hilde Domin: According to her, I said that Heidegger was scandalized regarding Röhm because he saw how much his expectations for a spiritual renewal were now false. Well then why, she asks, was he not scandalized, keeping the proper proportions in mind, regarding this thing that is infinitely more terrible and for us infinitely more shameful, which is the extermination that took place in the death camps? My response is that he was so scandalized by that thing that he was unable even to open his mouth. (*Turning to Philippe Lacoue-Labarthe*:) That is why it appears only in the context that you have illuminated in a critical fashion. . . .

PL-L: I'm afraid I don't quite understand.

H-GG: Well, let's take it up from your reading of Heidegger's text concerning "industrial production." That was, was it not, the only time he made any mention of this horror?

PL-L: To my knowledge, yes.

H-GG: And you are right. And at present this demands to be interpreted. I believe, for my part, that Heidegger was so obsessed by this vision, by the extent of this deviation and error of humanity, by the forgetting of being, he was so full of this vision that he did not open his mouth concerning this thing—which, naturally, on the moral and political level, is breathtaking and leaves us speechless. From there, I continue somewhat in the sense of what Derrida was suggesting; I am going in this direction by responding in this way regarding the interpretation of this single mention.

RW: There is still something very unsatisfying in this interpretation.

H-GG: No doubt. But that is precisely the point that Derrida insists on: it is fruitful because that mention remains unsatisfying and becomes an injunction to think.

PL-L: I can see the sense of your interpretation, but I maintain that, for me, that phrase remains shocking, since, on the other hand, there is no mention of Auschwitz. And since it is to my knowledge the only allusion to be found in his work, I find it shocking—although I understand perfectly what he meant to say— to place on the same level the extermination, motorized agriculture, blockades, and hydrogen bombs. If you like, it is not a question of interpreting the phrase, because at bottom, from the point of view at least of what I propose as a reading of Heidegger, this phrase is effectively correct, and I believe that, as you have said, it refers to a sort of immense distress—his own—, a distress, a pain that, for example, the fragments of the *Beiträge* published under the title "Overcoming Metaphysics" express several times, which is such a pain that one no longer even feels it. . . .[21] So I very much agree with you. But this laying out side by side of four phenomena, as if, implicitly, there were no hierarchy in these phenomena—that is what seems shocking to me. It is something that, on the one hand, raises a certain question, and on the other hand it strikes me as scandalous—that is the word I use.[22] One cannot say, without thinking it through any further, that the industrial production of corpses is the same thing as motorized agriculture.

PROF. HÜBSCHMANN: You spoke of the engagement of 1933. But we need an explanation of the seductive force that Nazism was able to have for Heidegger. You spoke of logocentrism: I would speak of a magic of words in Heidegger, and I would like to read a few lines that he addressed to his students in Freiburg on November 3, 1933:

> Let your loyalty and your will to follow be daily and hourly strengthened. Let your courage grow without ceasing so that you will be able to make the sacrifices necessary to save the essence of our *Volk* and to elevate its innermost strength in the State.
> Let not propositions and "ideas" be the rules of your Being.
> The Führer alone *is* the present and future German reality and its law. Learn to know ever more deeply: from now on every single thing demands decision, and every action responsibility.
> Heil Hitler!
> Martin Heidegger, Rector.[23]

You have also spoken of enthusiasm, of hope regarding Germany. But the question I am asking myself is precisely where this enthusiasm of Heidegger's came from, for the author Hitler. For after all, the latter wrote *Mein Kampf*, which is a manual of terrorism and lies! And it must not be forgotten that a hundred thousand copies of the book were published. Had he not read it? I ask myself what happened there and what were the causes of Heidegger's behavior. Is it an idealism at all costs? Even at the price of truth? The fear of communism? Perhaps our French friends can give us some kind of response about this. For it is a response that is also important for the present.

PL-L: I would merely like to bring in a precision, which is not a non-response. This text that you read is part of a group of texts that Heidegger explicitly disavowed in 1966, in the *Spiegel* interview. This is merely a precision because there are not very many gestures of that kind from Heidegger, so one finds it necessary to point this out. Concerning these texts, he expressed a regret. The only text for which he maintained responsibility is the rectoral address. That is all.

MICHA BRUMLIK:[24] It does not seem entirely admissible to me still to hypostasize Martin Heidegger's silence on the extermination camps as a kind of "plus" of his philosophy. Not, indeed, because it is not a particularly subtle turn of thought to extrapolate a positive element from something that perhaps did not even take place, but rather because, in fact and quite simply, it does not accord with the documents brought to light.

A few years ago, some letters from Herbert Marcuse to Martin Heidegger, written toward the end of the 1940s, were published.[25] It emerges there that Heidegger, in response to a question from Marcuse concerning his position on Auschwitz and the extermination camps, answered by referring to the bombing of Dresden. In the political domain, one could say that this is a mere settling of accounts, without much interest. However, we find here an implicit philosophical notion of some importance; and this implicit notion is the following: these industrial killings, here by airplanes, there in the gas chambers, reflect, in a certain way, the destiny of being, the *Gestell* ["enframing"] that through death takes on all power over men.

The problem I am posing is situated there: is it reasonable to "de-moralize"—in the strictly philosophical sense of "removing

from the field of morality"—such terrible events, that is, to elimi-
nate from them the concept of responsibility?

This leads me to pose a question to M. Derrida. You concluded your first intervention by saying that, given the current
situation of the world, it seems to you completely irresponsible to
defend, still today, a classical concept of individual responsibility.
I would only like to ask you to explain which concept, which reasonable concept of responsibility we should think of today, if not
that of guilt and will to action proper to each individual, on condition, of course, that this be in solidarity and reciprocity among all?

JD: If I were able to define this concept of responsibility in
one phrase, I mean to say, the one I am thinking of and the one
that in the end guides me, both in my work and in my questions
and my discourse, if I could do that, I would have done it.

I believe that the question of the response, of what responding means, responding to the other, responding for oneself,
responding *for* in general, is one of the most enigmatic questions
there is. I could make a lot of facile, coded statements—I have a
professional training that would enable me to put forth a long
discourse on responsibility, in Kantian terms, for example—, but
I believe that those discourses are insufficient for what we are
speaking of here. I do not believe that it is a question of replac-
ing one concept with another. It is not a question of saying that
responsibility, defined in terms of a categorical imperative, good
will, Kantian subject, that this is not sufficient, therefore we will
replace it with something else. No, that is not how this happens.

The definition of responsibility is not a theoretical act: responsibility is not something defined theoretically, it is something
taken, slowly, at length, indefinitely, incessantly—I mean to say,
constantly. And the fact that I do not have a response to give you
in the form of a phrase or a philosophical concept on this subject,
not only does that not mean that I am for the abdication of responsibility, or that I prefer irresponsibility, as some might hastily

accuse me of doing, but on the contrary it means that I believe
that the sharpest—I would not say the highest: that is precisely a
word I distrust, particularly in Heidegger—, the most demanding
of responsibilities imply that we must continue to do this work, for
example to interrogate the history of responsibility, the history not
only of speculative concepts but of the culture of responsibility.

When we debate here on Heidegger, that is one of the forms
of responsibilization. I believe that the way in which each one of
us comports himself or herself in this debate with regard to Nazism, with regard to the memory of Auschwitz, in the reading of
texts, in the manner of conducting, of engaging in a conversation,
and what one calls deconstruction, for example, all this is an exercise in responsibility. And it is not because deconstruction decon-
structs a received concept of responsibility that it is irresponsible.
On the contrary: I believe that it is an exercise of responsibility
to remain vigilant before the inherited concepts of responsibility. And it is a fact that the concept . . . let's say (I make use of this
word very rapidly, globalizing in my turn, and I ask you to forgive
me for it) . . . the metaphysical concept of responsibility, such as
it was formed throughout the history of philosophy, notably in its
Kantian moment, as it was inscribed in the rights of man, in the
democratic axiomatic, in Western morality and politics, that these
concepts, European concepts, did not prevent Auschwitz, did not
prevent Nazism. And even that, very often, Nazism, Nazi discourse,
used the very axiomatic that one opposes to it; that the countries,
the nations, the regimes, the politics and policies around Germany, between the wars, allowed it to happen, in a certain manner—and I am speaking not only of the cowardice of governments,
of armies, etc. There was, in discourses, in people's heads, something for which the theoretical concept and the form of injunction
of that responsibility were not sufficient.

Not only did it not constitute a sufficient defense against
Nazism, but it established a network of complicities of every sort,
in every dimension, to the point that what gives us all a bad con-

science today, what makes it such that people who speak in the name of the rights of man are so nervous, is that this concept of responsibility *is not sufficient.* That all the categories that it implies, that of the subject, of intention, of good will, are not sufficient. And if, when one speaks of psychoanalysis, of the unconscious, of psychiatry, one speaks of a lot of things for which the categories that we use are insufficient, and make it such that the juridical discourse that dominates our societies is absolutely powerless to measure up to what is happening in those societies—criminality, pathology, what is unfurling in the form of the military-industrial—, this means that our responsibility is to interrogate these concepts of responsibility that are not sufficient.

I do not have a response to give you in two words, and if I did have one we would not be here to work, all of us, for a long time now, and with difficulty, on the debates and the anxieties that you are aware of. I do not have the impression of abdicating responsibility by working on questions the way I do.

RW: Allow me to point out that we have been debating for four hours and that a certain fatigue is beginning to be felt, here at the table. That is why I would like to ask for one final question.

EBERHARD GRUBER: I would indeed like to continue the discussion, and I don't know whether everyone is tired, for I believe that now it's starting to become interesting. I would first like to continue in the same sense as Micha Brumlik, but by rereading what Philippe Lacoue-Labarthe has said.

I think that Heidegger's silence on the extermination, because he lacked the words, leads one to assume that he was against it. But one can read also in the other sense that he was not entirely against Auschwitz, *perhaps* (now I am playing devil's advocate), because he made no distinction between the victims: on the one hand the soldiers, on the other hand, the innocents in the extermination camps. I think therefore that, from the moment when Heidegger makes no distinction between the victims, he

does not see that he is not thinking what Lacoue-Labarthe calls the
essence of the West, which is founded on the exclusion *of* . . . :
of the Jews, of another religion, of another race. . . . And if one
refuses the notion that it is possible to assimilate the German
victims to the Jewish victims, one should also think that Heidegger
voluntarily kept silent on Auschwitz because he was not entirely
against it.

On this idea of the exclusivity of the West, and of the exclu-
sions that it provokes, one can then move, I think, to the question
of the totalitarian. And what Jacques Derrida said at the beginning was, in my view, very illuminating: one cannot critique the
totalitarian just anyhow. The legitimate critique of the totalitarian should itself be non-totalitarian. And here is posed, it seems
to me, the question of critique. A critique that strives to be real
always searches, I would say, for the smallest common denominator between the means of critique and the object of critique; the
smallest common denominator, because, if the critique has a larger
intersection with its object, it becomes affirmative and ideological; but if there is not at least a small denominator in common,
the critique misses its object and it becomes a quarrel between
opinions.

The question, then, is this: what is this smallest common denominator? My hypothesis is that it is a *relation.* That is to say that
critique cannot efface its object but can simply critique the internal
relations of the object; and therefore, in a certain manner, give
another image, another composition of the very object of critique.
Everything becomes therefore a question of order, of *Anordnung.*

And if one understands that the relation can be real only
when there are two *relata* that differ from one another, one can
read the relation inversely, as a difference. If one reads the difference as a real difference, one understands that the difference is
there really where there are supports that differ *for* one another.
That is why I believe that the problem of relation and the problem
of difference are two sides of the same question. And to come back

to the totalitarian, I would say that in order to critique the totalitarian it is necessary to think at the relational and differential level, and that it is necessary, in a certain manner, to look at how the differential works the relational, and how everything that is differential is linked together.

JD: I think I agree with what you just said at the end: to think the differential, that is what is at issue.

RW: All of this, I know very well, is very thought-provoking . . . but because we have gone far beyond the allotted time (it is after midnight) I really must close this discussion and thank the participants for having offered such weighty reflections in their improvisations.

HEIDELBERG, FEBRUARY 6, 1988

On February 6, the day after the conference, a meeting between the philosophers and part of the audience was organized at the Sole d'Oro restaurant in Heidelberg, in the presence of a number of journalists.

MEETING OF FEBRUARY 6, 1988

QUESTION: I would like to return to the notion of responsibility, but from another point of view. My question is addressed to Jacques Derrida and to Philippe Lacoue-Labarthe. You have presented your philosophical work as being, practically, an attempt at a new definition—considering the exhaustion and the general state in which we find the traditional definitions to which we have had recourse up to now. Allow me to ask you whether we might not also pose the problem of *your* responsibility, if not as philosophers at least as intellectuals, in the delay effect, in the

constrained and forced character (which you yourselves have
recognized) of the circumstances at once complex and somewhat
equivocal: the publication of the book by Farias. Can we ask you
why, finally, it is only now, when you are, as you said, "disarmed,"
that you have begun to speak about subjects concerning which
you describe at once the gravity and the painful character of the
discussions they bring with them? For by the same token you risk
the accusation, albeit excessive and caricatural, of speaking only
when constrained and forced, whereas you have at your disposal
a long established knowledge and a permanent aptitude to
speak out.

   JACQUES DERRIDA: This question is no doubt addressed more
directly to me, given what I said. Before trying to respond, one
remark. Since you are in fact posing to me the question of responsibility, I would like to recall, as I have already said, what troubles
me about the format of the discussion of Heidelberg: the public
spectacle, the simplifying constraints that that could produce; and
what troubles me regarding the philosophical ethics of putting
forward propositions that I knew would be simplifying and that,
because of the situation, would have a greater echo than what all
of us here would publish after weighing our words. So my request,
since some of those who are here are going to publish phrases,
or serve as a conduit for what we are saying, my request is the
following: I appeal to *your* responsibility to respect not only
what we say, but also what we do not say, that is, the precautions
that we take with regard to simplification. And if one must quote
a phrase spoken here in these conditions of improvisation, I ask
that one take account also of the work on the basis of which, for
half a century, for a quarter of a century, we have been trying to
confront and to explicate [*nous expliquer avec*] these responsibilities. Therefore, I too appeal to the responsibility of those who
practice your profession—which I respect, and which I believe is a

profession that is respectable in its mission, even if it is not always respected in its exercise.

That said, I will try to respond to you. First, I don't believe that what we are saying here, or have been saying for some time, about Heidegger and Nazism, [I don't believe that] we have said it because we were constrained and forced by the Farias effect. We said it in a certain way, at a certain rhythm, in a certain mode, for a certain time now. What the Farias effect precipitated, perhaps, is a certain modality of statements, and in certain places. Suddenly, indeed, we were obliged to speak of it in a certain mode, in places where we were not speaking of it up to now. But previously, anyone who wanted to know how we were exercising our responsibility—I say "we" here, in an abusive and simplifying way . . . but in any case your question is addressed especially to the French—, I believe that anyone who wanted to be interested in the question has been able, by reading the texts by Lacoue-Labarthe, by following his teaching, [they have been able] to know that, for twenty years, he was engaged in that work. And this is also the responsibility of those who do not read, who do not listen, who select, filter things, who speak of this book rather than that book, it is their responsibility in this silence. But in fact, there was no silence: there was the *non-perception* of a certain work. One can say this about the example of Philippe Lacoue-Labarthe, but also about other examples.

Why, nonetheless, knowing a certain number of things— since Schneeberger in 1962;[1] as for me, I knew since 1968 that Heidegger had kept his Nazi Party card; it was Beaufret who told me. Then there was the article by Hugo Ott, etc.—;[2] why did we work as we have done? Should we do something other than what we have done? Perhaps. I do not want to try to say, concerning myself, that what I have done is very good. I will try to explain why I believed I was doing the best possible in doing as I did. But, once again, it is not a self-justification. I will try to explain. Considering what I knew and what I was able to read in Heidegger's texts, it seemed to me more important—and this is a question of an economy of strengths, of means, of time—, it seemed to me economically more important, more urgent, to try to read Heidegger's texts as I am able to do, to teach Heidegger by searching in his text for a way to attempt to understand the relation there could be between the facts of his Nazi engagement and his text. And I thought that this was the best thing that I could do, and that it demanded patience, a great deal of patience. And that I was better exercising my responsibility by doing that than if I rushed to isolate these facts (by saying: I know that Heidegger was in the Nazi Party; or, in this or that work I learned this, and that is what is essential on the subject of Heidegger). I exercised that responsibility in light of the fact that the French scene was already prepared, and ill prepared, to receive this information. We know this having witnessed it on the occasion of Farias's book. For it is not the first time; there have been, already, episodes with Faye,[3] Fédier,[4] etc., when the problems were poorly posed and when it was a question, there too, of conjuring away what I believe it is responsible to consider as the ground of the problems. This amounted, then, to launching this information into a terrain that was already coded, already ready to conjure away the problems, to close the files—as one has tried to do again on the occasion of Farias's book.

I do not want here to go through all the accusations one could make against discourses put forth on the occasion of this book's appearance. . . . Fortunately, certain interventions stopped that movement. One tried to dispose of the problem, to say, we will no longer read Heidegger. I know that for me (perhaps Philippe will say something different), it was within my responsibility to do this work of reading Heidegger and of articulating these readings with others (I have been reading Heidegger for thirty years, but I am also interested in many other texts), and that it was in my view more urgent to do this work than to take up a microphone to announce what everyone was able to know (one

needed only to read), and so to contribute to the closing down of
the problem. From that point of view, I did what I was able to do;
if we were able to look more closely at the details, I could show
you more specifically what I am now saying in general terms.

As I was saying before, the definition of this responsibility is
very difficult for me. I cannot define it in moral or political terms
in the usual sense of these terms, because these terms are still,
for me, the names of open problems. Therefore, which responsibility am I obeying by doing this work that I do, in general, on
Heidegger? This is an open question. I know that I am obeying
something. The definition of this law, of this injunction, I do not
possess it in a philosophical form today. I know that Heidegger's
discourse on this subject does not satisfy me. It has helped me,
no doubt, to move from what we might call a Kantian type concept, intentionalist and voluntarist, of responsibility, to another
type of response—for Heidegger, the response that he gives of *Ruf*
and of *Gesinnen*, of originary *Schuldigsein*,[5] displaces the question of responsibility toward something other, toward the question
of being, and I know that it is by going in this direction, without
stopping there as Heidegger did, that one must redefine this responsibility.

I am saying these things too quickly, much too quickly, of
course. I believe that the question is one of responsibility, I believe
that the passage through the Heideggerian meditation on responsibility is an obligatory passage, it is a passage in which I have not
thought myself able to stop, and therefore the question of responsibility remains open. It is open for the future, but it is the future
of something that has already passed, that has set me underway
[*en chemin*] ever since I have been underway. It is this that makes
me understand. All this is not clear for me, but I do not at all have
the feeling of having failed (I have no doubt failed regarding some
responsibilities, I am not trying to say that what I have done is
very good), I do not believe that I have forgotten the sense of a responsibility that you would call ethical or political in that domain.

Even though I am also conscious of how all sorts of limits have prevented me from doing what I would have wanted to do—as far, as quickly, as forcefully, as fully as I would have liked—, but there too, the insufficiencies that I could describe, with regard to myself, on this score, I could describe them only by referring myself to a rule or to a law. And once again, that consciousness that I have of not having done enough (which you no doubt share with me!), that consciousness or conscience, I have it precisely because I listen to a certain injunction.

PHILIPPE LACOUE-LABARTHE: I will limit my comment to one type of responsibility, without neglecting what you were calling a political responsibility (far from it): this is the responsibility of work. Regarding this Heidegger affair, you rightly point out that we are here now obliged to respond to a certain pressure, and to respond to it according to means that are not ours, for example, the press or the radio, or the debate before a large gathering, to which we are not accustomed, if only, quite simply, in terms of its size, and the difficulty there is in articulating something before such an audience. If we are in this situation, it is because there is a certain urgency. I don't want to enter into an autobiographical narrative, but already when I was a student, at the very beginning of the 1960s, a first polemic on this subject already erupted in France— in reality it was the second, but for me it was the first. This was the publication by Jean-Pierre Faye of a translation of Heidegger's proclamations published by Schneeberger, and the responses that Fédier attempted to give, and then the polemic that had been set off essentially between the journals *Médiations* and *Critique*. At that time, when I was a student, it seemed to me that the problem was poorly posed, and that, from one end to the other, the work of translation on one side, and the justifications given by Fédier on the other, were avoiding the ethical and political problem, or a problem that was more than ethical and more than political, which was at the center of this polemic.

   Since that time, it has seemed to me that it belonged to the
responsibility of work [*du travail*] to take up this question, which
was extremely difficult. I waited until 1978 to approach it directly,
and I began by doing so in my teaching, maintaining the greatest caution, beginning first of all to read with the students the
properly political texts of Heidegger, then the texts following his
resignation. I tried to write about this. . . . What Jacques said is
completely justified: it happens that these texts are published, it
happens that in large part the conference at Cérisy that we organized, around the work of Derrida, was devoted to this question.
No one has ever spoken of it. I am not complaining, but that's
how it is. . . .

   JD: It's necessary to complain about it! Not for our sake. . . .
But that is the question! The work that we are evoking now, why
has the network of—let's call it the media, to speak quickly—why
did they not pick up on it? or pick up on it so little? That is a question. It is a question we are asking, not at a personal level, but as a
guiding thread for an analysis of the French situation for the last,
let's say, twenty or twenty-five years.

   PL-L: Quite simply, if you like, I have the impression that
this responsibility of work,—I, we, and not only we two, for there
are many other texts that have been written on this subject—we
have taken up this responsibility. But we have taken it up insofar
as this was a way to find the means to approach such a question,
through a reading that we hoped would be serious and in depth.
And not simply to arrive one day or another with this big news,
that Heidegger was a fascist. Which, philosophically speaking, has
only a very limited interest.
   If someone like Heidegger, that is to say, a thinker like Heidegger, was compromised, as one says, in this political history, this
poses an enormous question. And it is in relation to the enormity
of this question that, I believe, we have engaged our philosophical responsibility. Each one with his own means. But by trying not

to break a sort of rule of philosophical reading and of the rigor required in the formulation of questions. Now, of course, because of the situation that we have tried to describe a little, it happens that the debate on Heidegger has left the semi-academic circle in which it still remained in the 1960s. The material basis for this is no longer *Critique*, nor the now defunct journal *Médiations*; today it is based in the mass media, in newspapers and television. And we who are classified, from the outside and quite summarily, as "French Heideggerians," we see ourselves indeed forced to respond; our difficulty being that the response we are being pressed to give, we are now very afraid of having to give it much too rapidly, while simplifying things far too much, because we are being asked to respond with a yes or a no: you're either for or you're against. And this is where the true ethical problem, if you will, of responsibility is posed.

QUESTION: I would like for someone to explain to me why this discussion did not take place in German. Heidegger's philosophy has a lot to do with the German language, and Heidegger himself emphasized its philosophical importance. He even said that the Germans are a metaphysical people. In addition, when one wants to reflect on Heideggerian concepts, some of them are untranslatable, and I think that Lacoue-Labarthe and Derrida also read Heidegger in German. It was you, Professor Gadamer, who sent out the invitation, it is therefore to you that I would like to pose this question: would it not be more reasonable to treat this question of the philosophical and political dimensions of Heidegger's thought *in German*? Are we not dealing with a German philosopher, with a segment of German history, and isn't this encounter taking place in a German city?

HANS-GEORG GADAMER: The decision to speak French belongs to me. The reason for it is quite simply the current situation. When you see how in the blink of an eye, in France, all these things exploded somehow all at once, it becomes necessary to give our

French colleagues, who must reflect upon this situation, the best conditions possible for them to master the analysis to the greatest extent possible: and consequently for them to be able to express themselves in their own language. For our part, we [Germans] have had fifty years to do this; to reflect on these things that, in France, have just burst forth so suddenly.

My own life has been profoundly marked by all this. I would ask you not to forget that Guido Schneeberger already provided in the 1960s all of the important documents in this regard; and he did so with rigor and seriousness. The only thing that is really new today is the access to the archives of Meersburg, which allows us to have an interesting look into the situation in the university during National Socialism. This is what Farias's book shows us, since we did not have access to these archives. But, alas, one sees also how Farias's interpretations of these documents are unfortunate. For what he draws above all from these documents is how, in ten months, Heidegger failed in his struggle to have some influence on the cultural politics of the Third Reich in the region of Baden. That is obvious. Of course, the party tried to hijack and to exploit as much as possible the international reputation that Heidegger had acquired. That is why he received offers [*Berufungen*] from Berlin and from Munich—although we know today very precisely, and also through Farias's publication, that this was due to the influence of the party and not that of the university. Thus one learns, thanks to these archives, what sort of opposition within the university, in Freiburg, was taking shape against the calls from Berlin and from Munich, opposition that would finally lead to Heidegger's resignation. That is why Heidegger refused Berlin and Munich. He described this in very solemn terms in *Warum bleiben wir in der Provinz?*[26] But the real reason is that he had understood that he was undesirable. And that he was risking the same failure as in Freiburg with his concept of "cultural revolution," as it were, with his ideas of cultural revolution, which were not in accord with those of the Third Reich.

I had, of course, still another reason for deciding to speak French in Heidelberg, and it was the concern to recreate the same conditions of reception for our French guests as those that they themselves had extended to me during my stay in Paris a few years ago. For it was clear, at that time, that with our rudimentary French we would not be able even to dare to express ourselves or to appear on the scene . . . and so we therefore spoke German.

But of course you must also grant to the hermeneut that I am that it is possible to engage in a true dialogue only in a shared language, a language that is held in common.

QUESTION: Professor Gadamer, you were at that time at the University of Marburg. I would like to know how you lived this situation as a professor, and what you thought at that time.

H-GG: I have already touched on this question in part. And I confided some things that people, today, with some distance, might think strange. We felt an enormous surprise. We had been at Marburg already for a few years. Heidegger had left that university in 1928. Five years later, you know what happened then. We did not understand how that could be possible. That is of course our point of view, limited if you like, for we lived through this in a very different climate. And this climate that we were living in at Marburg was very deeply influenced by the Protestant Church, in particular by the position of the *bekennende Kirche* [confessing church] in the *Kirchenkampf* [church struggle]. I was also a close friend of Bultmann.[7] In short, this climate at Marburg was, from the start, extremely critical.

Beyond that, and I must here say this very explicitly, the philosophy faculty at Marburg, where Heidegger had had a position, found itself represented by a certain number of Jewish professors, brilliant and renowned, with whom we were closely connected. For me, any compromise with the Nazi Party was out of the question: it never even entered my mind, since for me, among these professors, there were my friends: Erich Freund, Erich Auerbach,

Jakobson, Paul Jacobsthal, who was an archaeologist . . . Paul
Friedländer had been my professor in classical philology.[8] In short,
even without having the least political motivation, there were
plenty of good reasons—those of friendship, of honesty, and of
fidelity to one's friends—to completely distance oneself from the
party. And in fact I was made to pay for this: I waited ten years
before being given a professor's chair at the university. Karl Löwith
was also one of my young colleagues at Marburg.[9] With him, too, I
remember very precisely how all that happened (don't think that I
want to defend myself, or to boast: I would like merely to respond
clearly): in 1933, I proposed to him that we use the informal form
of address. This was, I thought, a way of showing him my solidarity. You see, such was our situation at Marburg.

It was a terrible shock when Heidegger sent me the "rectoral address" with the inscription "mit deutschem Gruß."[10] I said
to myself that he had lost his mind! He had always concluded his
letters to me with "mit herzlichem Gruß" . . . and suddenly he was
writing: "mit deutschem Gruß"!! It was a shock; and for five years
I refused to see him. Until I was sure that he had freed himself
from that sort of engagement. And for all of us this was a normal
attitude. At Freiburg, no doubt, it must have been a little different:
the personality of someone like Heidegger and his force of persua-
sion must have made an impact. And many of his friends from that
period, honorable people it must be said, such as Erik Wolf, for
example, the jurist, rallied behind Heidegger unconditionally.[11] It's
astonishing.

MILAN CHLUMSKY: Can the principle that in French is called
"*responsabilité*" be the same as what in German one calls "*Verantwortung*"? In German, "*Verantwortung*" means that there is first,
implicitly, an action that provokes a reaction, and this reaction is
finally *Verantwortung*; that is, from the outside, I myself am called
upon to respond to things I can do nothing about.

PL-L: We are constrained to responsibility, is that what you mean?

MC: No, I mean that in French and in German responsibility is necessarily something different.

PL-L: But responsibility, in French, is also a response.

JD: Yes. One responds *for* [*on répond* de]. Then, after that, one can reappropriate the origin of the response, but the response assumes first of all that the movement comes from the other, from over there. I am—from the point of view of a responsible being— a finite being, since I am situated in such a way as to respond to a call or to a provocation or to a situation that this being has not chosen—that somehow *chooses him*, that comes to him. Responsibility, from this point of view, is indeed always secondary, even if the possibility of this secondarity assumes—one always forgets this—a freedom. That is to say, the fact that I can make myself the origin of the response to something of which I am not the origin. But in French as in German, responsibility supposes response. So, to whom does one respond? What is a response from this point of view? What is a response that, in some way, precedes the question?

Here we return to the question of the question, of which we have already spoken at some length. It happens that Heidegger, for a very long time, defined the question beyond science, beyond philosophy, as the very dignity of thought, as piety, *Frömmigkeit*. Somehow he never placed in doubt that questioning was thought itself in its highest dignity. Which went together despite everything—even though all this was not for him simply metaphysics, science, philosophy—with the motif of the quest, of an investigation [*enquête*], of a search for principles, for causes, etc. And then, in the text *Unterwegs zur Sprache*, he says something like, "when I said that questioning was piety . . . it was more complicated." He does not say, I was wrong, I made a mistake, but, it was more complicated. First, he explains what he meant by *fromm* [pious],

which did not simply mean piety in the religious sense, but the
reference to the Greeks, the fact of being, in advance, already docile; *docile* means he who listens, who is obedient. Therefore, to
pose a question it is not only necessary to be active, it is not only
necessary to have the initiative of activity: questioning is already a
listening—a listening to but also of or from the other. I do not have
the initiative, even of the question, even in this piety of thought
that is the question.

But then comes the discourse on the *Zusage*, according
to which there is, in fact, *before* the question, so to speak—in a
logical or chronological before—more originary than the question, there is this *Zusage*, this acquiescence, this confidence: this
consent to *die Sprache* [language] without which there would
not even be a question.[12] Therefore I have said a certain yes, even
before questioning. Then there is the question of translation.
One can say "trust," "consent"—not "passivity." But for there to
be questioning, however active it may be, there must nonetheless
be this attunement to *die Sprache*—which one cannot translate
either, neither by "language [*langue*]," nor by "speech [*parole*]."
If there is *Zusage*, if one places oneself at this point of the *Zusage*, that in my opinion modifies, re-forms the entire itinerary
previously followed by Heidegger—he does not contradict it, but
this obliges him to re-form everything that he had said about the
authority of the question—, then at that moment one has another
access to responsibility (I am returning to your question). Heidegger spoke all the time about responsibility, responding to
the call of being: there would be no responsibility if there were
not, already, the call of being that is not the call of someone, of a
god. . . . I am, even before responding in terms of moral conscience, I am accountable, responsible for a call that comes to me,
I know not from where. It is not God; it is not another consciousness or conscience. I am imputable. Dasein is a responsible being,
that is, a being that must respond to a call that already constitutes
it. But from that moment, which is the moment of *Sein und Zeit*

and of the years that followed it, under the authority of the question, at the moment of the *Zusage*, there is already a displacement of the motif of responsibility. Always the motif of responsibility: I am responsible before even knowing for what, or before
whom. It remains to me to know to what, to whom the *Zusage*
will be directed. It is there that the political risk of the *Zusage* is
very serious. For it is one thing to say, from the moment I am in
die Sprache, in discourse, from the moment I speak, I say yes in
a certain way (there is a yes that is anterior, Rosenzweig said this,
an originary yes);[13] it is one thing, then, to recognize in this yes
an absolutely originary responsibility, which I cannot escape, and
it is another thing then to determine to what and to whom I say
yes when, at that moment, I accept being responsible for this or
that, before this or that instance or authority. It is there that the
matter is determined politically: between the *Zusage* in general
and then the acquiescence to this or that juridico-political instance for this or that act. . . . There is a step, and this step *is* the
step of what we call "juridico-political," which is at once ineluc-
table and undecidable: because it is necessary to traverse the moment of undecidability.

   In other words, often, in the French situation that we were
evoking a moment ago, and also in other places that are not
French, one accuses for example those who practice a deconstructive discourse, a French-style discourse, those who pass through
difference, the undecidable; one says to them, but this is a politics
of neutrality, of indifference, of indecision. . . . And I say *exactly
the contrary*: there is no possible responsibility that does not
undergo the ordeal of this undecidability, and of this impossibil-
ity. I believe that an action, a discourse, a behavior that does not
traverse this ordeal of the undecidable, with all the double binds,[14]
all the conflicts of which one could give examples, is simply the
tranquil unfolding of a program—more or less tranquil. The program can be Nazi, democratic, or something else . . . but if one

does not traverse this terrifying ordeal of undecidability, there is
no responsibility. It is along this path that I seek that for which and
before which I will feel responsible.

PL-L: I would like to add something, for, in my opinion, this
does not say quite enough: it is after all explicitly in the name of
this originary responsibility that Heidegger took a side, politically,
historically. One can find, and one does find in general, that the
declarations in which Heidegger explained himself concerning
his own behavior are very weak. Moreover, one finds that they are
deceitful. Nonetheless, in every case they recall very clearly that
in 1933 it was a question, for him, of taking a risk. That he was
perfectly conscious of the leap he was making between, let's say,
something like the call of being and the leap it was necessary to
take in order to become committed. And it seems to me that it is
only on this basis that one can envisage the question of his engagement. Not otherwise.

QUESTION: Philippe Lacoue-Labarthe recalled that there had
been a gesture of Heidegger in the interview he gave to *Der
Spiegel*, which consisted in repudiating all the political texts of the
period of 1933 except the "rectoral address." I would like to know
what the import of this gesture is in your view, of this repudiation;
and what is the difference, at that moment, between the "rectoral
address" and the other texts.

PL-L: The repudiation has this form, if I recall correctly:
"today I would no longer write such things."

INTERVENTION: That is quite weak, in any case. It is insufficient.

PL-L: I am not saying that it is sufficient. But one does not
have the right to pass over this proposition in silence and to
leave it unanalyzed. Farias never mentions it. On the other hand,
this negative proposition, however feeble and insufficient it is, is

accompanied all the same by a vindication of the rectoral address. Therefore, it does mean clearly, despite everything, that it is in the rectoral address that his engagement effectively occurs, and that one finds the real reasons given for this engagement. Consequently, Heidegger indicates that there is also a certain weakness in having pronounced the other texts that were printed in student newspapers. That is why this repudiation is important all the same: it amounts to a recognition on his part that he should not have done that.

QUESTION: The rectoral address is not a Nazi text. It is not at all national-socialist. The concept of race does not exist, the word "Jew" is not found in it, "Führer" in reference to Hitler does not exist. Hitler is not mentioned. It does not even speak of the greatness of the German nation. He does not even speak of Versailles, of a revenge to be had (which everyone thought at that time), there is not even any anti-Marxism. Not a word. It is a question of something completely different: the reform of the university.

M. Gadamer spoke of the particular situation that was dominant at Marburg. Do you think, Professor, that it would be possible to imagine that Heidegger, if he had stayed in Marburg, would not have become a Nazi because of the Protestant atmosphere? Is it true that at Marburg, which was Protestant, Heidegger played the Catholic, that is, in philosophy, of the scholastic, whereas one studied neither Aristotle nor St. Thomas there? He did that deliberately, didn't he? Whereas at Freiburg, he played the Protestant, or rather the anti-Catholic. And I think that his engagement in Nazism lies in large part in his anti-Catholicism: because Heidegger is, at bottom, what one would call a "defrocked priest."

JD: I believe that Heidegger's anti-Catholicism, his anti-Christianism, is something that has always appeared to me extremely false, very much a denegation.

H-GG: I think that we have to nuance a bit. It's true what you say about Freiburg, about the return to Freiburg that renewed, naturally, his resistance against the clergy, against the imperialism of the church, against this entire social system based on the Catholic Church. But the description that you give of his activity and of his own understanding of himself at Marburg is different. There, he had become more or less Protestant. He studied Luther already in 1922. He wrote an introduction to Aristotle that began with Luther. And the entire development of Bultmann is already influenced by Heidegger.

Your remark on the form in which he tried to formulate his adherence to Hitler while avoiding the dogmatisms of the party is completely true. And if you study it word for word, you can see how he tried to avoid the things that he refused. In the publication of his courses also, one sees how he always attacked biologism, Nazism, anti-Semitism. That was in his courses, even during the war. Personally I was much freer at Leipzig because no one was interested in me, but Heidegger, naturally, was very exposed as a member of the party. To be sure, the secret police also came to my courses . . . but the only result was that they didn't understand a word!

PL-L: When you say the rectoral address is not Nazi, I don't think that one can say it so simply. It does not obey the watchwords of Nazism, but it is Nazi in the sense of the truth of Nazism according to Heidegger's terms. And in particular—but it would be necessary here to have the text in order to read it very attentively—on the question of anti-Marxism. There is an entire development that explains that the workers, this is not a class but a state (*Stand*). Which is meant to be a rectification of the figure of the worker as it appears in Marxism.

You said that the address is not anti-Semitic: indeed, there are no explicit anti-Semitic statements in it, just as there are none, to my knowledge, in the texts written and pronounced by Hei-

degger. Nonetheless, there is a development on spirit (*Geist*),
which is not intellectual curiosity, which is not *Witz*, which it
seems to me has very clear connotations, if not narrowly anti-
Semitic at least anti-intellectual.[15] One does after all find the
phrase *Blut und Erde* . . . Heidegger never said *Blut und Boden*,
but he displaced the formula.[16] It's a displacement that anyone can
read through. There are also a number of things that would have
to be brought out by looking closely at the text. There is a whole
strategy that Heidegger employs in relation to the ready-made
phrases of Nazism; there is an entire elaboration, very refined and
always very tricky, in relation to certain stereotypes. But all the
same, these stereotypes are apparent.

JD: That is why this text of the address is a gem to be studied
for years. For there are at least three gestures, in this text, that are
extraordinarily complicated. On the one hand, there are concessions to the demands of the situation with Nazi hegemony. There
is also a gesture made to adjust these concessions—without them
appearing as concessions—to the strategy of Heidegger's discourse
in its own coherence (*Sein und Zeit* and other texts in which he
had already developed his own thought). And then, after that,
there is a German tradition that is very old and deep, in which all
the themes of the rectoral address were already hammered out
since the beginning of the nineteenth century, by all the discourses in philosophy concerning the university. Indeed, someone
who could think (especially in France, I imagine) that it's possible
to decipher straightaway the rectoral address by opening it and
immediately denouncing the things that are there, saying that it
is flat, that it is the text of a rector in a certain situation, would be
making an error that is not only philological but also philosophical: he would understand nothing about it. This text is unreadable
on a first reading, without a preparation that would pass through
a political reading of the German situation at that moment—which
is already very difficult—, a knowledge of Heidegger's earlier texts,

and then a serious knowledge of . . . Hegel, Fichte, Schelling, Nietzsche. . . .

H-GG: Yes, especially Fichte.

QUESTION: The essential points have already been raised. But all the same, in that context, for all those who were listening to Heidegger at that moment, the connotations of words like *Aufbruch, Sturm, Bewegung, Volk* . . . :[17] one cannot deny that this was a Nazi discourse. For those who heard it at the time, but also for those who read it today and who indeed know a little about the history of all these words, this text can only be understood as a Nazi text. There are nuances, of course. And the ministry did in fact sense at the time that it was a sort of displaced Nazi ideology, Heidegger's private version. But the effect of the address, for those who heard it, was absolutely clear: it emanated, at that moment, from a partisan of National Socialism.

JD: But it was not only the *effect* of the address: it was the *fact* of the address, of the situation, etc. That is why I think it is a discourse with a false bottom [*à double fond*].

H-GG: I would propose calling Heidegger, in truth, a National-Bolshevik. That is not simply a joke. You know that Farias's book also tried, among other things, to indicate this point of view, and it presented some sources on the relations between the student committees and the Röhm Putsch. I already emphasized this: Röhm, certainly, was not a racist in the sense Hitler intended. I am absolutely sure that if Hitler had chosen Röhm and not Göring, then the extermination camps would not have existed.

QUESTION: I am surprised that no one here is talking at all about Sternberger's analysis of the specific language of this discourse, of Heidegger's language.[18]

H-GG: Of course, you are right. I wanted only to note that Heidegger, in the eyes of the dogmatic party members, had been a heretic. But that is the only thing that one can say.

QUESTION: I would like to pose a question regarding this time of an undecidability to be crossed. First, those of us who think that it is necessary to cross it are in the minority. When one is a young philosopher, it is necessary also to mark the disarray in which one finds oneself in relation to the new model that you propose in contrast to what one could call, grosso modo, a communicational type model. Concerning this time of undecidability: we know very well that it must be crossed and that it must be done because that is already the first moment of action, and therefore the first moment of political reality. But I wonder all the same how to cross it while escaping what Lacoue-Labarthe calls a mimetology—that is, how to pass through this moment of undecidability without adhering, *despite everything* (and I emphasize the word), to a will to myth—or something of that order? It seems to me that one of the responses that one could offer is to work on the question of identification, and that as long as we don't define or redefine what, perhaps, we have always understood and misunderstood by identification, we will not be able to exit this problem in a valid way.

JD: These are very difficult questions, which would demand another rhythm of meditation. I will only draw out a few features, very elliptically. First, I do not think that undecidability is a time— that is, that there is a step to be taken, that there is a time for undecidability, then a time for going beyond the undecidable. I believe precisely that the structure of this ordeal of undecidability has a much more enigmatic relation with time. If one could say to oneself that there is a time for undecidability and a time for deci- sion . . . that would be very simple. In short, the question of time is posed; this is something I can only recall here. A question of time and of non-time, of the instant. The problem is that responsibility is taken—and this is what is undecidable—even before time is given, in a certain way. . . . Here I am only complicating the question that you have posed.

Next, for the very important question of mimetology and identification, I will say, in a somewhat elliptic or aphoristic way, that there is responsibility only if identification is ruptured, which is impossible. You used the word "model": no, there is no model. The problem is this: a truly singular responsibility, one that would truly be *my* responsibility, but *mine* in a sense that does not refer to an ego or a possession, my singular responsibility can be a singular responsibility only if, naturally, I break with every model and every identification. . . . I don't know if that is possible. In another sense, there is no responsibility that can be taken without an identificatory reference. This is one of the aporias of responsibility. All the same, there is an identification that ends up being worked out. I do not know how one can simply transgress the law, or if it is necessary to transgress it in order to open the field of responsibility. That is a question.

PL-L: As I see it now, I don't believe in the possibility of a transgression of the law of imitation or of the law of identification. But it seems to me, perhaps, that a certain ordeal of responsibility would consist in an interruption, in letting imitation be interrupted, or in the acceptance of a certain collapse, perhaps, of identification—which seems to me at once very difficult to think and a sort of ordeal, itself even more difficult. Based on what I tried to do for one of the great questions that we are faced with, I believe that it is the possibility of the introduction of myth. And it is precisely, more and more, perhaps, the question of myth in Heidegger that interests me. When I say myth, I translate in the sense of *mythos* everything that he tried to articulate around *Sage*, while of course he also set aside *saga* with a very confident gesture.[19] But when he says *Sage*, he is referring, all the same, to explicit statements on the mechanism of identity and national

identity. Homer gave the Greeks their gods, and therefore the
Greeks depend on Homer; the Greeks are an effect of Homer. Just
as the Germans could have been an effect of Hölderlin if they had
listened to him. So I believe that there is here an enormous question that it is necessary to work on—one cannot decide it just like
that—and that one of the stakes of Heidegger's thought and one of
the new questions, especially because of his last texts, like *Unterwegs zur Sprache*, for example, is this: can one, is there a possibility, first of all, to think the renunciation of myth? But this has
nothing to do with what has been called "demythologization." It's
something completely different.

JD: I would just like to add one point. It seems to me, for
example, that the work that Lacoue-Labarthe is doing on the question of identification, of mythology and politics in Heidegger, is
certainly one of the most fruitful paths for posing the question of
the political in Heidegger and in his texts. In saying this, I want
to emphasize that there is here a responsibility to work, a will
to work, that is taken on. I am specifying this in order to correct
slightly what I said before when I spoke of the mediatic filter that
had its responsibility in the situation evoked by the question at the
beginning. My response was insufficient, for two reasons. First, because it may have implied that it was the responsibility of particular journalists. (I am not saying that this is something I don't have
to talk about, but it is itself possible only against the background
of a more general structure of the cultural and intellectual press in
its relations with the university, which it would also be necessary
to analyze, in longer and shorter sequences.) On the other hand,
and it is here that my response was insufficient, one would have
to push the same work in the direction of the university, for there
is the same filter, and sometimes in a great complicity between
the press and the powers at work in the university; the same
filter has been and continues to be guilty of the same discrimina-
tion. I could give many examples that would show that some of

the works we are speaking of now not only were not recognized, legitimated, or evaluated, presented, or even summarized in the various outlets of the French press, but neither were they in the university where, for often analogous reasons, the same effects were produced. This is therefore often the case: there is a certain field where one finds united the hegemony of the university, the powers at work in the university, *and* a structural hegemony of intellectual power that finds expression in the press. An analysis, and not only a sociological analysis, should be applied to the articulation of these two domains. It is there that the responsibilities of everyone are called.

Jacques Derrida concludes with thanks:

JD: We thank you for the hospitality, we thank especially Professor Gadamer for this hospitality, which is above all his own, since we are in his city, in his university . . . and in our language.

APPENDIX: "LIKE PLATO IN SYRACUSE"

Hans-Georg Gadamer

The uproar that Victor Farias's book has provoked in France is quite surprising. Could it be that so little is known there about the Third Reich? Heidegger's followers, believing they were defending him, no doubt contributed to the affair by continually repeating the refrain of his "rupture" with Nazism at the end of a year of disappointing experiences as the rector of Freiburg. In German-speaking countries, almost all of what Farias reveals has long been known. His zealous archival work does more to illuminate the bureaucratic procedures of the years following Hitler's seizure of power than to provide any new point of view. Here no one is able to feign surprise in discovering that Heidegger did not leave the Nazi Party (which, since the appearance of Farias's book, some have taken pleasure in presenting as the latest news).

To be sure, the younger generation in Germany, too, finds it difficult to imagine the reality of that time: the conformism, the pressure, the ideological indoctrination, the sanctions. . . . Many of them ask, "Why did none of you cry out?" Let us say first of all that one often underestimates the natural human inclination toward conformism, which is always ready to be taken in by any type of deception. Wasn't the height of this deception the following question: "Does the Führer know about this?" In the spring of 1934, those in academic circles, including even my Jewish friends, still maintained a hope that anti-Semitism, for example, had been no more than a tactic of electoral politics—albeit a terrible one—that "the drummer" (as Hitler was called at the time) had used quite crudely. When in May 1934, in Marburg [German vice-chancellor Franz von] Papen gave his speech, written by [Edgar] Jung, we saw in it only a much-awaited hope for the end of the revolution and a return to the rule of law.[1]

Another strategy consisted in explaining, out of admiration for the great thinker, that his political errors had nothing to do with his philosophy. No need to worry! No one even noticed how insulting such a "defense" was for such a significant thinker. And how was this distinction to be reconciled with the predictions that this same Heidegger made, beginning in the 1950s, concerning the industrial revolution and technics, which today are astonishing in their foresight?

In any case, having reflected for fifty years on the reasons that disturbed us back then and separated us from Heidegger for many years, we cannot be astonished (this is the least one can say) to hear that in 1933—and in fact well before, and for how many years after?—he "believed" in Hitler.

Heidegger was not a mere opportunist. His political engagement clearly did not have much to do with political reality. The dream of a "people's religion" encompassed, in fact, his profound disillusionment at the course of events. But he secretly safeguarded this dream. This is the dream he believed he was pursuing during the years 1933–34, convinced that he was rigorously fulfilling his philosophical mission by attempting to revolutionize the university. It was to this end that he did everything that outraged us. For him it was a question of breaking the political influence of the church and the inertia of the academic mandarins. He even gave Ernst Jünger's vision of "The Worker" a place alongside his own ideas on overcoming the tradition of metaphysics on the basis of being. Later, as is well known, he went so far as to speak of the end of philosophy. That was his revolution.

Did he then feel no responsibility for the terrible consequences of Hitler's seizure of power, the new barbarism, the Nuremberg laws, the terror, the blood spilled—and, finally, the indelible shame of the extermination camps? [The answer is a rigorous "no." For that was the perverted revolution and not the great renewal arising from the spiritual and moral [*sittlich*] strength of the people, which he dreamed of and longed for as the preparation of a new religion of humanity.]

I am sometimes asked whether, after these "revelations" (which for us were no such thing), one can "still even today" get involved as before in the philosophy of this man. "Still even today"? Whoever asks this question has a lot of catching up to do. What was considered the world over as a radical step forward in thought, his confrontation [*Auseinandersetzung*] with the Greeks, with Hegel, and finally with Nietzsche, had all this suddenly become false? Or have we long since finished with all that? Or perhaps what we are being asked to do is definitively to renounce thinking.

Watching anxiously from afar as Heidegger thus strayed into the cultural politics of the Reich, we sometimes thought of what happened to Plato at Syracuse. One of his Freiburg friends, seeing him in the tram after his departure from the rectorship, asked him, "Back from Syracuse?"

Despite considerable research, and despite the information it provides, Farias's book is very superficial and has long been outmoded, and this is very regrettable. But when it enters into the philosophical domain, its superficiality becomes grotesque, and it simply overflows with ignorance.

The requirements of thinking are not so easily eluded. Even those who were disturbed at the time by Heidegger's political adventure and distanced themselves from him for many years would never have dared to deny the philosophical impetus with which he had not ceased to inspire them from the beginning. [Just as Heidegger in the 1920s did not create blind followers for himself, likewise one must find one's own paths of thought, now more than ever.]

[Whoever believes that today one need no longer be concerned with Martin Heidegger has not taken the measure of how difficult it will always be for us to debate with him, instead of making oneself ridiculous by looking down on him with an air of superiority.]

NOTES

FOREWORD
Jean-Luc Nancy

[Except where otherwise indicated, and in some cases where bibiographical information for texts in English has been added, all notes are those of the editor of the French edition.]

1. [Nancy's phrase here is "antisémitisme historial." He is referring in part to Peter Trawny, *Heidegger and the Myth of a Jewish World Conspiracy*, trans. Andrew J. Mitchell (Chicago: University of Chicago Press, 2015), where Heidegger's term *seinsgeschichtlich* is translated literally as "being-historical." Elsewhere Nancy has used the word "historial" both in this sense and for the German word *weltgeschichtlich* ("world-historical," which one also finds in Heidegger); see especially Nancy, *Banalité de Heidegger* (Paris: Galilée, 2015) (an English translation of this text is forthcoming from Fordham University Press). With this double meaning in mind, I retain here Nancy's term *historial.*—Trans.]

2. [The distinction Nancy points to here and in what follows cannot be rendered clearly in English. Whereas *Sein*, being (or Being), is often translated into French with an article (*l'être*), translations of this term into English tend to drop the article; use of the definite article in English ("the being") usually refers rather to "beings" or entities (*das Seiende* or, in French, *l'étant*). The title of Heidegger's major work, *Sein und Zeit*, contains no articles.—Trans.]

PREFACE
Reiner Wiehl

1. That debate, organized by Philippe Forget, took place at the Goethe Institute in Paris, from April 25 to April 27, 1981.

2. Victor Farias, *Heidegger et le nazisme* (Paris: Verdier, 1988); English: *Heidegger and Nazism* (Philadelphia: Temple University Press, 1991).

EVENT OF THE ARCHIVE
Mireille Calle-Gruber

1. [*Auseinandersetzung* is a term that Heidegger used to describe (notably with respect to Nietzsche, among others) a respectful but agonistic confrontation with a thinker through close analysis. The word implies conflict in the sense of "having it out" with someone or entering into something in order to bring out what is implicated in it—hence its translation into French as "explication," in the sense of an interpretive unfolding, a term that will be rendered literally in what follows.—Trans.]

2. Gadamer's "Collected Works" (*Gesammelte Werke*; hereafter GW) were in the process of being published: from 1985 to 1995 they appeared in ten volumes with Mohr Siebeck (Tübingen). By 1988, *Warhheit und Methode* (1960) had been in part translated into French by Étienne Sacre and Paul Ricoeur (Paris: Seuil, 1976). The first English translation appeared as *Truth and Method* (New York: Seabury Press, 1975).

3. See Philippe Lacoue-Labarthe and Jean-Luc Nancy, *Le Mythe nazi* (La Tour-d'Aigues: L'aube, 1991). See also the American version, published in English, at the University of Chicago Press: "The Nazi Myth," trans. Brian Holmes, *Critical Inquiry* 16 (Winter 1990): 291–312.

4. Jacques Derrida, "La circonfession," in Geoffrey Bennington and Derrida, *Jacques Derrida*, "Les contemporains" series (Paris: Seuil 1991), 53; English: "Circumfession," in Bennington and Derrida, *Jacques Derrida*, trans. Geoffrey Bennington (Chicago: University of Chicago Press, 1993), 52.

5. Published in French as "Bonnes volontés de puissances (Une réponse à Hans-Georg Gadamer)" and "Et pourtant: puissance de la bonne volonté (Une réplique à Jacques Derrida)," in *Revue Internationale de Philoso-*

phie, no. 151 (1984): 341–43 and 344–47, respectively. Gadamer's text
was translated into French by Philippe Forget from the original German,
which first appeared in Philippe Forget, ed., *Text und Interpretation*, UTB
1257 (Munich: Fink Verlag, 1984). Derrida's text was transcribed from
the recording of the colloquium. [The texts appeared in English with the
shortened titles "Three Questions to Hans-Georg Gadamer" and "Reply to
Jacques Derrida," in *Dialogue and Deconstruction: The Gadamer-Derrida
Encounter*, ed. Diane P. Michelfelder and Richard E. Palmer (Albany:
State University of New York Press, 1989), 52–54 and 55–57, respectively.
—Trans.]

  6. Lacoue-Labarthe, *Heidegger, Art and Politics*, trans. Chris Turner (Ox-
ford and Cambridge, Mass.: Basil Blackwell, 1990), 46 [translation slightly
modified].

  7. Ibid., 44–45.

  8. See Gadamer's text in the Appendix: "Like Plato in Syracuse"; see also
Jean Grondin, "La rencontre de la déconstruction et de l'herméneutique,"
in *Philosopher en français*, ed. Jean-François Mattei (Paris: PUF, 2001),
235–46. A chronology of the encounters between Gadamer and Derrida is
provided there. For more details, see Jean Grondin, *Hans-Georg Gadamer:
A Biography*, trans. Joel Weinsheimer (New Haven: Yale University Press,
2003).

  9. Martin Heidegger, *Überlegungen II–VI* ("Schwarze Hefte," 1931–38),
Gesamtausgabe (GA) 94; *Überlegungen VII–XI* ("Schwarze Hefte," 1938–
39), GA 95; *Überlegungen XII–XV* ("Schwarze Hefte," 1939–41), GA 96; ed.
Peter Trawny (Frankfurt am Main: Klostermann, 2014). The *Schwarze Hefte*
or "black notebooks" are named after the color of their covers.

  10. See Karl Jaspers, *Philosophische Autobiographie* (Munich: Piper,
1977), chap. 10, "Heidegger." The book was published in a new edition
including this new chapter on Heidegger (after the latter's death), 92–111;
esp. 101: "Es gibt noch eine gefährliche internationale Verbindung der
Juden" ("But there is a dangerous international alliance of Jews").

  11. Peter Trawny, *Heidegger und der Mythos der jüdischen Weltver-
schwörung* (Frankfurt am Main: Klostermann, 2014); English: *Heidegger
and the Myth of a Jewish World Conspiracy*, trans. Andrew J. Mitchell (Chicago: University of Chicago Press, 2015). [Mitchell's translation renders the
term *seinsgeschichtlich* literally as "being-historical"; I have here followed

the French text with a literal rendering of the term *historial*. See the translator's note to Nancy's Foreword.—Trans.]

12. See Hugo Ott, *Martin Heidegger: Unterwegs zu seiner Biographie* (Frankfurt am Main and New York: Campus, 1988).

13. Derrida, "Wie recht er hatte: Mein Cicerone Hans-Georg Gadamer," *Frankfurter Allgemeine Zeitung*, March 23, 2002. This text was translated into French by Jean Grondin: "Comme il avait raison! Mon Cicérone Hans-Georg Gadamer," in *"Il y aura ce jour . . .": A la mémoire de Jacques Derrida*, ed. Georges Leroux, Claude Lévesque, and Ginette Michaud (Montreal: Editions à l'Impossible, 2005), 53–54; reprinted in *Contre-jour*, no. 9 (2006): 87–91.

14. Ibid., 54.

15. See Derrida's statement on page 35.

16. Gadamer, "Et pourtant: Puissance de la bonne volonté," 347; English: "Reply to Jacques Derrida," in *Dialogue and Deconstruction*, 57; quoted by Jacques Derrida in "Comme il avait raison! Mon Cicérone Hans-Georg Gadamer," 56.

17. A touching detail: Derrida always confused the dates of Heidelberg, referring, both in his private correspondence and in the publication of "Rams," not to February 15, 2003, but to "February 5, 2003"—which corresponds to the date of the conference in 1988.

18. Derrida, "Rams: Uninterrupted Dialogue—Between Two Infinities, the Poem," in *Sovereignties in Question: The Poetics of Paul Celan*, ed. Thomas Dutoit and Outi Pasanen (New York: Fordham University Press, 2005).

19. Paul Celan, *Atemwende* (Frankfurt am Main: Suhrkamp, 1967), 93. An English version of the poem, beginning "Great, glowing vault," can be found in Celan, *Breathturn*, trans. Pierre Joris (Los Angeles: Sun and Moon, 1975), 233.

20. Derrida, "Rams," 161.

21. Ibid; Derrida's emphasis.

22. Gadamer, *Lesen ist wie übersetzen* ("Reading is like translating"), in GW 8:279–85. Gadamer had published a commentary on this poem by Celan: *Wer bin ich und wer bist du? Kommentar zu Paul Celans Gedichtfolge "Atemkristall"* (1973; repr. Frankfurt am Main: Suhrkamp, 1986); English: "Who Am I and Who Are You?" in *Gadamer on Celan: "Who Am I and*

Who Are You?" and Other Essays, by Gadamer, ed. Richard Heinemann and
Bruce Krajewski (Albany, N.Y.: SUNY Press, 1997), 67–126.

23. Gadamer, "Grenzen der Sprache," GW 8:350–51; English, "The
Boundaries of Language," trans. Lawrence K. Schmidt, in *Language and
Linguisticality in Gadamer's Hermeneutics*, ed. Lawrence K. Schmidt
(Lanham, Md.: Lexington, 2000), 16 (translation modified); quoted by
Derrida in "Rams," 138.

24. I would also like to thank Anaïs Frantz and Olivier Henry, research
assistants at the Université de la Sorbonne Nouvelle–Paris 3.

25. Lacoue-Labarthe and Nancy, *Le mythe nazi*, 16. [This quotation is
from the very end of a preface added by the authors to the 1991 edition of
the essay in book form and is therefore not found in the Holmes translation
published in *Critical Inquiry*.—Trans.]

CONFERENCE OF FEBRUARY 5, 1988

1. Karl Jaspers, *Philosophische Autobiographie* (Munich: Piper, 1977).
The French translation by Pierre Boudot, *Autobiographie philosophique*
(Paris: Aubier, 1963) does not include the chapter on Heidegger, which was
not published until after the latter's death. Jaspers (1883–1969) was forced
to leave his position as professor of philosophy at the University of Heidelberg from 1933 to 1945, in the face of disapproval regarding his marriage to
Gertrud Mayer, a German Jew. He was Hannah Arendt's thesis director.

2. Hans-Georg Gadamer, "Like Plato in Syracuse"; see the Appendix.

3. Karl Löwith, *Mein Leben in Deutschland vor und nach 1933* (Stutt-
gart: Metzler, 1986); English: *My Life in Germany Before and After 1933:
A Report* (Champaign-Urbana: University of Illinois Press, 1994).

4. Letters written in November 1978 and January 1979; see *Le Monde*
of January 8 and January 22, 1988.

5. Lacoue-Labarthe, *Heidegger, Art and Politics*, 95.

6. [Gadamer is referring to the first publication of Derrida's essay "Ousia
et Grammé" in an edited volume dedicated to Beaufret, *L'endurance de la
pensée: Pour saluer Jean Beaufret* (Paris: Plon, 1968). The essay was later
reprinted in Derrida's book *Marges de la philosophie* (Paris: Minuit, 1972);
English: *Margins of Philosophy*, trans. Alan Bass (Chicago: University of
Chicago Press, 1982).—Trans.]

7. Martin Heidegger, "Die Zeit des Weltbildes" (1938) in *Holzwege*, GA 5; English: "The Age of the World Picture," in *Off the Beaten Track*, ed. Julian Young and Kenneth Haynes (Cambridge: Cambridge University Press, 2002), 57–85.

8. Gadamer, "Like Plato in Syracuse"; see the Appendix.

9. Article of Walter van Rossum, "Wie braun war Heidegger?," *Die Zeit*, November 6 1987.

10. Ludwig Klages (1872–1956), psychologist and philosopher, favored "life" in opposition to "spirit," defended a tendency toward a form of Germanic mysticism.

11. Luc Ferry and Alain Renaut, *La pensée 68: Essai sur l'anti-humanism contemporain* (Paris: Gallimard, 1985); English: *French Philosophy in the Sixties: An Essay on Antihumanism*, trans. Mary H. S. Cattani (Amherst: University of Massachusetts Press, 1990).

12. Derrida, *De l'esprit* (Paris: Galilée, coll. "La philosophie en effet," 1987); English: *Of Spirit: Heidegger and the Question*, trans. Geoffrey Bennington and Rachel Bowlby (Chicago: University of Chicago Press, 1989).

13. Heidegger, *On the Way to Language*, trans. Peter D. Hertz (San Francisco: Harper Collins, 1971).

14. See, for example, Heidegger, "A Dialogue on Language," which bears the subtitle "Between a Japanese and an Inquirer [*ein Fragender*]," in Heidegger, *On the Way to Language*, 1–54. [Derrida here says "*questionnante*," "questioning" not as a noun but as an adjective modifying *la pensée* (thinking).—Trans.]

15. Derrida is probably thinking of "Das Wesen der Sprache" (1957), translated as "The Nature of Language," in *On the Way to Language*, 57–108, where Heidegger concludes (108) by invoking "the breaking up of the word" (*das Zerbrechen des Wortes*) in order to lead back to the "way of thinking" (*Weg des Denkens*).

16. Derrida, *Margins of Philosophy*, trans. Alan Bass (Chicago: University of Chicago Press, 1982); first published in French in 1972.

17. [See Nancy's Foreword and the translator's note appended to it. —Trans.]

18. "Zur Seinsfrage" (1955), initially written for a collection published in honor of Ernst Jünger and entitled, "Über die Linie" ("On the Line" or "Over the Line"); English: "On the Question of Being," trans. William

McNeill, in Heidegger, *Pathmarks*, ed. William McNeill (Cambridge: Cambridge University Press, 1998), 291–322 (concerning the crossing out of "being," see especially 310–14).

19. Ibid., 311. Concerning the "fourfold" (*Geviert*), see also Heidegger, "Building Dwelling Thinking" (1951) (in *Poetry, Language, Thought*, trans. Albert Hofstadter [New York: Harper and Row, 1971]) for the relation between the four: "earth and sky, divinities and mortals" (*Erde und Himmel, die Göttlichen und die Sterblichen*) (147).

20. Hilde Domin (1909–2006), German Jewish writer and poet, exiled in Italy and then in the Dominican Republic until her return to Germany (Heidelberg) in 1954. Recipient of numerous literary prizes, including the Rilke Preis (1976), the Nelly Sachs Preis (1983), the Hölderlin Preis (1992).

21. See Heidegger, "Überwindung der Metaphysik," in *Vorträge und Aufsätze* (Pfullingen: Neske, 1954); English: "Overcoming of Metaphysics," in *The End of Metaphysics*, trans. Joan Stambaugh (New York: Harper and Row, 1973).

22. See Lacoue-Labarthe, *Heidegger, Art and Politics*, 34.

23. "German Students (November 3, 1933)," in *The Heidegger Controversy: A Critical Reader*, ed. Richard Wolin (Cambridge, Mass., and London: MIT Press, 1993), 47.

24. Micha Brumlik (b. 1947), a philosopher at the time, is professor emeritus of education at the Goethe University of Frankfurt am Main. From 2000 to 2005 he was director of the Fritz Bauer Institute for the Study and Documentation of the History of the Holocaust.

25. Letters from Herbert Marcuse to Martin Heidegger of August 28, 1947, and May 13, 1948, in which Marcuse refers to a letter from Heidegger dated January 20, 1948. For an English translation of the letters, see "An Exchange of Letters: Herbert Marcuse and Martin Heidegger," in *The Heidegger Controversy*, 160–64.

MEETING OF FEBRUARY 6, 1988

1. Guido Schneeberger, *Nachlese zu Heidegger: Dokumente zu seinem Leben und Denken* (Bern: Suhr, 1962).

2. Derrida is probably referring to Hugo Ott, "Wege und Abwege," in *Neue Zürcher Zeitung*, November 27, 1987. The article was translated into

French: "Chemins et fourvoiements," *Le Débat*, no. 49 (March–April 1988): 185–89.

3. See Jean-Pierre Faye, "Martin Heidegger: Discours et proclamations," and "Heidegger et la 'Revolution,' " *Méditations* (Fall 1961): 139–50 and 151–59.

4. See François Fédier, "Trois attaques contre Heidegger (Guido Schnee-berger, Theodor W. Adorno, Paul Hühnerfeld)," *Critique*, no. 234 (November 1966): 899–901.

5. It is a question of thinking responsibility as a response to a "call" (*Ruf*), to an originary "being-guilty" or a "being-in-debt" (*Schuldigsein*), and to a "perfective sense, prior to the senses and to their performative orientation" (*Gesinnen*), as if one could think only by rethinking *Ruf*, *Schuldigsein*, and *Gesinnen*. Let us recall that this last term derives from *Sinn* ("sense"), from *sinnen* ("to meditate, to reflect") and from Old High German *sinnan* ("to take a direction, to tend toward, to journey"), all associated with the perfective prefix "ge-."

6. Martin Heidegger, "Why Do I Stay in the Provinces? (1934)," in *Heidegger: The Man and the Thinker*, ed. Thomas Sheehan (Chicago: Precedent, 1981), 27–30.

7. Rudolf Bultmann, a theologian inspired by the historico-critical method of liberal theology, is the author of *Glauben und Verstehen*, which appeared in 1933 with a dedication to Heidegger; translated into English as *Faith and Understanding* (Philadelphia: Fortress Press, 1987). Bultmann's thought sought to recover the original Christian message, separated from Catholic dogma, and found in the existential analysis of *Being and Time* a philosophical framework that allowed him to articulate a thought according to which the discourse on God bears on human existence (see "What Does It Mean to Speak of God," in *Faith and Understanding*). The confessing church was opposed to the Nazism of the "German Christians."

8. Paul Friedländer, a specialist in Plato studies at Marburg, practiced an immanent reading of Plato's *Dialogues*. Gadamer participated in his advanced seminar and worked with him to develop the idea of "dialogical ethics" in philosophy. As part of the work required for his state examination in classical studies, Gadamer also took Paul Jacobsthal's seminar on archaeology. Erich Auerbach, professor of romance philology at Marburg until 1935, was stripped of his functions by the Nazi regime, then forced to

emigrate first to Istanbul, then to the United States, where he was professor at Yale until his death in 1957. He is the author of *Mimesis: The Representation of Reality in Western Literature*, written in Istanbul between May 1942 and April 1945, published in Berne in 1946. Speaking of his "professor friends," Gadamer is no doubt referring to Bultmann's *Graeca* reading group, which he attended for fifteen years until his departure from Marburg, in 1939, as well as the circle of the *Graeca juniorum* created by Friedländer. As Gadamer's biographer Jean Grondin emphasizes, what was being transmitted here was not only a training in the tradition of humanism, but a true "form of life"; see Grondin, *Hans-Georg Gadamer: A Biography*, especially chap. 7, "Flight to the Greeks," 109–27.

9. Karl Löwith (1897–1973) undertook his habilitation work with Heidegger the same year as Gadamer, in 1928. When Löwith took up a teaching position in social philosophy at Marburg, Gadamer became his assistant, and did not take up his own teaching position until August 1933. Following the Nuremberg racial laws, Löwith was forced to emigrate in 1935. He is the author of *Mein Leben in Deutschland vor und nach 1933: Ein Bericht*. Written in 1940, the work was published posthumously (Frankfurt am Main: Fischer, 1989); English: *My Life in Germany Before and After 1933*, trans. Elizabeth King (Champaign-Urbana: University of Illinois Press, 1994).

10. The inscription "mit deutschem Gruß" ("with a German greeting") was the phrase used by the Nazis instead of the usual "with a cordial greeting." According to Jean Grondin, Gadamer did not see Heidegger during the period of the rectorate, in 1933–34, and then not until 1937 (he attended his lectures on "The Origin of the Work of Art" in November 1936 in Frankfurt am Main, but did not meet with him personally). He did not visit him in the Black Forest until summer 1937; see Grondin, *Hans-Georg Gadamer: A Biography*, chap. 9.

11. Erik Wolf (1902–77), professor at the University of Freiburg im Breisgau, dean of the faculty of law under the rectorship of Heidegger. In the second half of the 1930s, Wolf drew closer to the confessing church (*Bekennende Kirche*) after having published pro-National Socialist works in 1933–34.

12. *Die Sprache* is "the house of being" (*das Haus des Seins*) as a modality that is deployed between its unfolding as "speech" (*Rede*) and

its precondition, *die Sage* ("saying"). Between these two, it is a matter of "acquiescence" (*Zusage*).

13. Franz Rosenzweig (1886–1929), in Part 1 of *Der Stern der Erlösung* (1921), translated in English as *The Star of Redemption*, trans. Barbara E. Galli (Madison: University of Wisconsin Press, 2005), evokes the "originary word" (*das Urwort*), *Yes*, as "the negation of the nothing" (37): it "gives to every word in the sentence its right to existence, it offers it the chair where it may sit, it 'sets.' The first Yes in God establishes the divine essence in all infinity. And the first Yes is 'In the beginning.'" (35).

14. ["Double binds": in English in the original.—Trans.]

15. *Witz*, derived from *wissen*, "to know." The adjective *witzig* designates a play of wit, an acute form of intelligence—hence, at times, an anti-intellectual connotation.

16. "Blood and soil" (*Blut und Boden*) is a stereotype of Nazi language.

17. [These words mean, respectively: *irruption, storm, movement, people*.—Trans.]

18. See Dolf Sternberger, Gerhard Storz, and W. E. Süskind, *Aus dem Wörterbuch des Unmenschen* (Hamburg: Claassen, 1957). Sternberger (1907–89) was a political scientist; in 1931 he completed a doctoral thesis on Heidegger's *Being and Time* with the theologian Paul Tillich.

19. For Heidegger *Sage* designates the movement of poetry and thinking (*Dichten und Denken*) toward the "thinking word" (*Essais et conférences* [1954], trans. A. Préau [Paris: Gallimard 1976], 276). *Sage* conjoins three senses of the term: "fable" or *Dichtung* (the "Dict"); "making appear, showing"; the imperative of *sagen*, of naming ("Name!")—a conjuncture to which "speech" (*Rede*) corresponds and responds.

APPENDIX: LIKE PLATO IN SYRACUSE
Hans-Georg Gadamer

This article was published in French in *Le Nouvel Observateur*, January 22–28, 1988, in a translation by Geneviève Carcopino. We have restored in brackets certain passages that were omitted from the article in *Le Nouvel Observateur*. [Gadamer's text was published in German under the title "Zurück von Syrakus?," in *Die Heidegger-Kontroverse*, ed. Jürg Altwegg (Frankfurt am Main: Athenäum, 1988), 176–79. This text was translated into

English as "Back from Syracuse?," trans. John McCumber, *Critical Inquiry* 15, no. 2 (Winter 1989): 427–30. Note that the present text, even with the material that the French editor has restored in brackets, omits a number of passages that are found in the German version and in the McCumber translation. What is provided here is a faithful translation of the text as published in French, which Gadamer refers to during the conference.—Trans.]

1. [The French and English translations both have May, but the German text contained in *Die Heidegger-Kontroverse* correctly gives the date as June.—Trans.]